How To Write
QUALITY
EISs and EAs
SECOND EDITION

The
Shipley Group
Training • Consulting • Writing Services

The Shipley Group wishes to acknowledge the contributions and insights of the many Federal and state employees whom we have trained in NEPA procedures. Many of the principles and examples in this manual are adaptations of actual EISs and EAs written by these employees.

More specifically, we are indebted to the Boise National Forest for information and graphics related to effects analysis. We are indebted to Alaska Region (Juneau) of the Forest Service for procedures related to the analysis file (planning record). We also have used sample passages from many actual EISs and EAs written to comply with NEPA. We have edited or changed these sample passages, so any errors in fact or problems with the intent of a passage are the sole responsibility of The Shipley Group, not of the Federal agency or department producing the original EIS.

Authors: Larry H. Freeman, PhD
                  Sidney L. Jenson, PhD

Contributors: Roger Bacon, PhD
                  Alan Payne, PhD
                  Richard C. Moore

Design/Layout: Denise Decker
                  Patti Ferrin
                  Barbara Petersen

Proofreader: Camille West

Cover Design: Rosalie Dickson

The Shipley Group, Inc.
1584 South 500 West, Suite 201
Woods Cross, UT 84087
Phone (888) 270-2157
Fax (888) 270-2158
www.shipleygroup.com

200104
Printed in the United States of America

ISBN 0-933427-19-0

About The Shipley Group

The Shipley Group's Mission

Our mission is to help professionals **effectively interpret and skillfully communicate** legally essential environmental information. We provide government and private clients with consulting, training, and writing services so they can accurately analyze environmental effects and effectively communicate their findings to an agency decisionmaker and to the affected and interested public.

We define *environmental* to include professional work dealing with the *human environment*—the physical, biological, economic, and social environments.

Almost all interpretations and communications have legal implications. The simplest analysis or most technical document can lead to a legally debatable issue. Our mission is to help you effectively gather data, interpret those data, and skillfully communicate those interpretations.

Effectively Interpret (Analyze)

Environmental professionals must collect and interpret complex and seemingly contradictory data. Too often these data and their interpretations only weakly support agency decisions. Sometimes managers unintentionally encourage professionals to interpret data within an organizational culture that fosters bias.

We at The Shipley Group believe that objectively and effectively interpreting data and then clearly communicating these interpretations are inseparable tasks. Thus, all our consulting activities, training programs, and all of our writing, editing, and reviewing services address both interpretation (analysis) issues and communication skills.

We comply with NEPA (National Environmental Policy Act) by integrating the interpretation (analysis) and the documentation as concurrent, parallel processes. Our more than two decades of experience have proven that environmental professionals should start a project with (1) a well-defined analysis process, (2) a clear sense of the decision to be made, and (3) a concrete vision of the final documents.

Skillfully Communicate

Credit for scientific insight goes to the person who can skillfully communicate this insight. Once published, an insight must be validated by peer review and replication of the analysis process. Without publication, no public validation is possible.

We at The Shipley Group believe in skillful communication because it is both professionally important and legally essential under NEPA and other environmental laws and regulations.

Skillful communication, both written and oral, must be honest and clear. Honesty in all acts of communication is critical because if the honesty of the writer or speaker is questioned, credibility vanishes and communication ceases. Clear communication is critical because ambiguity and confusion cause misinterpretations. Our goal at The Shipley Group is to help you write and speak so that you cannot be misunderstood.

Shipley Environmental Services

Training Services

- Overview of the NEPA Process
- How to Manage the NEPA Process and Write Effective NEPA Documents
- How to Manage the Environmental Impact Analysis Process (USAF EIAP)
- Reviewing NEPA Documents
- Risk Communication: Strategies and Implementation
- Statements of Work for Environmental Projects
- Construction Specification Writing
- Preparing Statements of Work
- Clear Writing for NEPA Specialists
- Applying the NEPA Process within DoD Acquisition Programs
- Understanding and Preparing Preliminary EIAP Documents
- Writing for Technical Specialists
- Public Speaking
- Overview of the Endangered Species Act
- Improving Professional Communication
- Cultural and Natural Resource Management
- Interdisciplinary Team Building

Consulting Services

- Reviewing NEPA documents for consistency, adequacy, and compliance
- Facilitating internal and public scoping meetings
- Facilitating coordination of interagency NEPA documents
- Acting as intermediary for cooperating agencies
- Creating action plans for NEPA documents
- Creating internal and external communication strategies
- Implementing early intervention in NEPA actions
- Providing guidance in writing and presenting risky information
- Assisting with strategic planning
- Providing "Red Team" services for NEPA document review
- Providing guidance in the development of statements of work

Writing Services

- Writing NEPA documents (EAs, EISs, FONSIs, RODs, CEs/CATEXs, etc.).
- Developing communication strategies
- Revising and editing environmental documents
- Providing "Red Team" services for document review
- Preparing client policy and procedure materials
- Developing environmental and business communication training materials
- Preparing client on-line environmental documentation
- Reviewing, revising, and editing statements of work
- Writing environmental training modules
- Preparing communmication plans

CONTENTS

PRELIMINARY INFORMATION

PREFACE 1

BUILDING ORDER INTO ANALYTIC EISs/EAs 2

SUGGESTED CONTENT FOR AN EIS/EA 4

RECOMMENDED FORMAT 8

PARTS OF AN EIS/EA

COVER SHEET 12

SUMMARY 14

TABLE OF CONTENTS 16

PURPOSE OF AND NEED FOR ACTION (CHAPTER 1.0) 18

ALTERNATIVES INCLUDING THE PROPOSED ACTION (CHAPTER 2.0) 25

AFFECTED ENVIRONMENT (CHAPTER 3.0) 36

ENVIRONMENTAL CONSEQUENCES (CHAPTER 4.0) 46

LIST OF PREPARERS (CHAPTER 5.0) 61

LIST OF AGENCIES, ORGANIZATIONS, AND PERSONS TO WHOM COPIES OF THE STATEMENT ARE SENT (CHAPTER 6.0) 62

APPENDICES 64

INDEX 65

GLOSSARY 66

BIBLIOGRAPHY 67

RESPONSE TO COMMENTS 68

• Contents

OTHER NEPA DOCUMENTS

FINDING OF NO SIGNIFICANT IMPACT (FONSI) AND
DECISION NOTICE/DECISION RECORD (OPTIONAL) 70

RECORD OF DECISION 75

NOTICE OF INTENT 77

CATEGORICAL EXCLUSION 79

ANALYSIS FILE (PLANNING RECORD) 81

APPENDICES AND INDEX

APPENDIX A—SAMPLE OUTLINES FOR AN EIS OR EA A–1

APPENDIX B—A COMPLIANCE CHECKLIST FOR AN EIS OR EA B–1

INDEX I–1

PREFACE

For over 30 years, Federal agencies, the courts, and the public have been working to make the NEPA (National Environmental Policy Act) a reality.

NEPA is a law of disclosure. Agencies must disclose to decisionmakers and the public what society gains or loses with each decision. Well-written, analytic NEPA documents are essential to full and honest disclosure.

Despite progress, environmental analysis remains a difficult, inexact science. The human species' thirst for resources and ability to pollute exceed each prior year's predictions and projections. With such an unpredictable and uncontrollable human environment, few are confident in current environmental forecasts; many are ready to go to court.

As the framers of NEPA foresaw, population growth and nonrenewable resources would make trade-offs and compromise inevitable and difficult. Section 101 of NEPA speaks of the necessity for society and its decisionmakers to balance competing demands.

In the following pages, we suggest ways for you to make your NEPA documents better and more faithful to the NEPA mandate for a clear balancing of demands. Although our focus is on better documents, much that we say will apply to NEPA and the NEPA process. (For those of you who are primarily interested in NEPA or the NEPA analysis process, we recommend the The Shipley Group training course "How to Manage the NEPA Process.")

The following pages contain frequent cross-references to the *Franklin Covey Style Guide,* Third Edition (Salt Lake City, UT: Franklin Covey, Co., 1997). All cross-references use the abbreviation *FCSG* and the name of an entry in the *FCSG*.

The discussions on the following pages are complete enough, however, that you need not refer to the *Franklin Covey Style Guide.*

NEPA and its case law mandate a full and honest disclosure of all environmental impacts.

PURPOSE

Sec. 2. The purposes of this Act are: To declare a national policy which will encourage productive and enjoyable harmony between man and his environment; to promote efforts which will prevent or eliminate damage to the environment and biosphere and stimulate the health and welfare of man; to enrich the understanding of the ecological systems and natural resources important to the Nation; and to establish a Council on Environmental Quality.

—*The National Environmental Policy Act of 1969, as Amended*

BUILDING ORDER INTO ANALYTIC EISs/EAs

Follow the CEQ format for your EIS/EA.

Follow the organization that the CEQ (Council on Environmental Quality) strongly recommends for EISs (Environmental Impact Statements). For consistency, follow a similar (somewhat streamlined) format for EAs (Environmental Assessments).

Remember, however, to distinguish between the contrasting legal roles and processing requirements for EAs and EISs. Although both documents use a similar format, the EIS process requires the following:

- Early scoping with the public and other agencies (beginning with a Notice of Intent in the FEDERAL REGISTER)

- Circulation of a DEIS (Draft EIS) to all interested publics and agencies

- Publication of a FEIS (Final EIS) that directly responds to all substantive comments on the DEIS

In contrast, public scoping for an EA is optional (depending upon agency procedures); an EA usually does not circulate in a draft version; and an EA need not formally respond to public or agency comments. In some cases, other agencies and the public only learn about an EA when an agency publishes a notice that it has prepared a FONSI (Finding of No Significant Impact), based on an EA. See pp. 70–73 for a discussion of the FONSI and its role documenting decisions about the possible significance of impacts.

1. CEQ's recommendations are important because the current CEQ Regulations (1992) reflect many of the crucial case law decisions concerning compliance with NEPA. NEPA and the CEQ Regulations combine to form the legal framework for compliance with the law.

   We recommend that you obtain a full copy of the CEQ Regulations (40 CFR Parts 1500–1508, as of the 1992 reprinting) for reference purposes. In the following pages, however, we do quote from the most relevant sections in the Regulations.

2. The CEQ Regulations are well known and widely used. Lawyers, judges, and the public expect to see CEQ's recommended organization.

   In the following pages, we discuss CEQ's recommended content. We also make suggestions for organizing individual chapters and subsections. Our suggestions follow several basic principles for organizing and writing well-designed, consistent, and analytic EISs/EAs.

3. Chapters 1 and 2 (1: Purpose of and Need for Action and 2: Alternatives Including the Proposed Action) present managerial information to the decisionmaker and any interested publics. These two chapters usually contain almost everything a decisionmaker needs to know.

CHAPTER 1 + CHAPTER 2 =
AN EXECUTIVE SUMMARY

4. Chapters 3 and 4 (3: Affected Environment and 4: Environmental Consequences) present technical and scientific support for the managerial information in Chapters 1 and 2.

5. As section 1500.4 of the CEQ Regulations mandates, significant (relevant) environmental issues guide the internal order of all sections of an EIS/EA. Nonsignificant issues (resources) also have a role in an EIS/EA, but discussions of nonsignificant issues should be as concise as possible.

   Issue-oriented EISs/EAs will automatically be analytic rather than encyclopedic.

6. A well-written and carefully edited EIS/EA has clear summaries, section overviews, and other helpful editorial features. Without such features, readers are likely to be overwhelmed by resource data and technical analyses.

7. The interdisciplinary team must agree, as early as possible, on a detailed outline for the entire EIS/EA. All specialists should then follow this detailed outline when they prepare their technical discussions.

8. The interdisciplinary team should also prepare a full page-by-page mockup as early as possible. Use this mockup to plan how each page will look, including any visual aids. (If done well, a mockup will replace the detailed outline suggested above in point 7.)

9. An EIS/EA is a disclosure summary, with legally important supporting information in the appendices and the analysis file (planning record).

10. Although both an EIS and an EA are disclosure documents, they have different legal roles when they are contested. In a contested EA, the agency preparing an EA has to prove with its documentation that no significant impacts might occur. In a contested EIS, the burden of proof shifts to the public or another agency, who must prove that the agency preparing the EIS overlooked something or failed to follow the EIS process. A well-prepared EIS is, therefore, much easier to defend in court than an EA.

See the discussion of the analysis file on pp. 81–84.

CHAPTER 3 + CHAPTER 4 = SUPPORTING INFORMATION

CEQ REGULATIONS

§ 1500.4 Reducing paperwork.

Agencies shall reduce excessive paperwork by:

    (b) Preparing analytic rather than encyclopedic environmental impact statements (§ 1502.2(a)).

    (g) Using the scoping process, not only to identify significant environmental issues deserving of study, but also to deemphasize insignificant issues, narrowing the scope of the environmental impact statement process accordingly (§ 1501.7).

NOTE: Throughout this manual, all quoted sections from the CEQ Regulations appear in boxes like this one.

SUGGESTED CONTENT FOR AN EIS/EA

Sections with an asterisk (*) are usually retained in an EA; the others are omitted or combined with other sections.

*Cover Sheet (How to Read this EIS/EA)

NOTE: Add a *How to Read this EIS/EA* to the back of the Cover Sheet or perhaps in a separate card that can serve as a bookmark for the document. This guide should tell readers that Chapters 1 and 2 are an executive summary and that Chapters 3 and 4 contain supporting information. As appropriate, refer readers to special pages in the EIS/EA (for example, the Chapter 2 matrix that compares the effects of the alternatives). If you choose the card option, consider placing either a list of alternatives or a glossary of key terms on the back of the card.

NOTE: This content outline does not give the suggested headings for chapter subsections because the headings in an EIS or EA must change to reflect the features of each specific project.

Summary
Table of Contents
Issue Tracking Matrix

*1.0 Purpose of and Need for Action

*1.1 Explain **who** wants to do **what** and **where** and **why** they want to do it. Include project objectives.

*1.2 Explain any other EISs/EAs that influence the scope of this EIS/EA.

*1.3 Explain the decision(s) that must be made and identify any other agencies involved in this NEPA analysis.

*1.4 Summarize the scoping and explain the relevant issues. As appropriate, identify issues considered but discarded from detailed analysis.

*1.5 List Federal permits, licenses, and entitlements necessary to implement the project.

1.6 Preview the remaining chapters of your EIS/EA, especially if you have changed the CEQ organization.

*CHAPTER 1 + CHAPTER 2 =
AN EXECUTIVE SUMMARY*

* 2.0 Alternatives Including the Proposed Action

*2.1   Explain that this chapter describes the alternatives (potential actions). Also remind readers that this chapter summarizes the environmental consequences of the alternatives.

*2.2   Describe the alternatives, including the proposed action and no action. Your descriptions should focus on potential actions, outputs, and any related mitigations.

2.3   Explain how these alternatives represent a range of reasonable alternatives. As part of this explanation, describe briefly the alternatives eliminated from detailed study and explain why they were eliminated.

*2.4   Compare the alternatives by summarizing their environmental consequences and, as appropriate, their achievement of objectives. Potential actions and outputs would cause these consequences.

2.5   Identify your agency's preferred alternative, unless your agency directs otherwise. Do not give in the EIS/EA the rationale for your choice. Include the rationale in the ROD (Record of Decision) or Decision Document/FONSI.

Alternatives are the heart of the NEPA process. A range of reasonable alternatives shows the trade-offs facing the decisionmaker.

CHAPTER 3 + CHAPTER 4 = SUPPORTING INFORMATION

3.0 Affected Environment

3.1 Explain that this chapter presents relevant resource components of the existing environment—that is, the baseline environment. As appropriate, preview the chapter contents so that readers can readily find subsections.

3.2 Resource X (Issue 1)

3.3 Resource Y

3.4 Resource Z (Issue 2)
. . .

The subheadings in Chapters 3 and 4 reflect separate resources, but these resource discussions should reflect the scope of the relevant issues presented in Chapter 1 (section 1.4).

NOTE 1: Include **all** relevant physical, biological, social, and economic features of the human environment. Use the same order or sequence of resources in Chapters 3 and 4.

NOTE 2: Relevant issues (resources) should receive more extensive discussion than issues that are not relevant. For tracking, cross-reference resources with the relevant issues.

*4.0 Environmental Consequences (organizational option 1)

*4.1 Explain that this chapter is organized by resources.

*4.2 Effects on Resource X (Issue 1)
4.2.1 Alternative A (No Action)
4.2.2 Alternative B (Proposed Action)
4.2.3 Alternative C (Short Title)
4.2.4 Alternative D (Short Title)

Choose organizational option 1 if you have an EIS or a lengthy EA.

*4.3 Effects on Resource Y
4.3.1 Alternative A (No Action)
4.3.2 Alternative B (Proposed Action)
4.3.3 Alternative C (Short Title)
4.3.4 Alternative D (Short Title)

*4.4 Effects on Resource Z (Issue 2)
. . .

See Appendix A (pp. A–1 to A–8) for specific examples of how to organize Chapters 3 and 4.

*4.10 Unavoidable Adverse Effects
*4.11 Relationship of Short-Term Uses and Long-Term Productivity
*4.12 Irreversible and Irretrievable Commitments of Resources
*4.13 Any Other Disclosures

*4.0   Environmental Consequences (organizational option 2)

*4.1   Explain that this chapter is arranged by alternatives.

*4.2   Effects of Alternative A (No Action)
    4.2.1   Resource X (Issue 1)
    4.2.2   Resource Y
    4.2.3   Resource Z (Issue 2)
    . . .

*4.3   Effects of Alternative B (Proposed Action)
    4.3.1   Resource X (Issue 1)
    4.3.2   Resource Y
    4.3.3   Resource Z (Issue 2)
    . . .

*4.4   Effects of Alternative C (Short Title)
    4.4.1   Resource X (Issue 1)
    4.4.2   Resource Y
    4.4.3   Resource Z (Issue 2)
    . . .

*4.10 Unavoidable Adverse Effects
*4.11 Relationship of Short-Term Uses and Long-Term Productivity
*4.12 Irreversible and Irretrievable Commitments of Resources
*4.13 Any Other Disclosures

5.0   List of Preparers

*6.0   List of Agencies, Organizations, and Persons to Whom Copies of the Statement Are Sent   (For EAs, call this chapter the List of Agencies and Persons Consulted.)

Index

Appendices (if any)

NOTE: Some other sections can be either one of the appendices or a separate chapter:

Scoping Information

Bibliography

Glossary (Terms, Abbreviations, and Acronyms)

Maps

Choose organizational option 2 if you have a short EA or if you want to emphasize alternatives.

The key NEPA categories in sections 4.10, 4.11, and 4.12 are essential for adequate disclosure in an EIS. The Shipley Group also recommends disclosing them in an EA.

RECOMMENDED FORMAT

SUGGESTIONS FOR WRITING

Recommended Format

1. Follow the recommended format for both EISs and EAs. The amount and complexity of detail and the organization of the sections will be somewhat different in the two documents; however, in most situations the basic format should be the same because the purpose and logic of the documents are similar.

Consistency in format helps readers because they are familiar with the parts and will know where to look for the information they are interested in.

2. For short 10- to 15-page EAs, you might alter the format and combine sections. Retain, however, the essential CEQ content and terminology.

3. Name and number the sections of your EIS/EA as follows. Arabic numbers for chapters are now becoming more common than Roman numerals, but the

Follow the CEQ format unless a "compelling reason" makes another format more desirable.

CEQ REGULATIONS

§ 1502.10 Recommended format.

Agencies shall use a format for environmental impact statements which will encourage good analysis and clear presentation of the alternatives including the proposed action. The following standard format for environmental impact statements should be followed unless the agency determines that there is a compelling reason to do otherwise:

(a) Cover sheet.
(b) Summary.
(c) Table of contents.
(d) Purpose of and need for action.
(e) Alternatives including proposed action (sections 102(2)(C)(iii) and 102(2)(E) of the Act).
(f) Affected environment.
(g) Environmental consequences (especially sections 102(2)(C) (i), (ii), (iv), and (v) of the Act).
(h) List of preparers.
(i) List of Agencies, Organizations, and persons to whom copies of the statement are sent.
(j) Index.
(k) Appendices (if any).

If a different format is used, it shall include paragraphs (a), (b), (c), (h), (i), and (j) of this section and shall include the substance of paragraphs (d), (e), (f), (g), and (k) of this section, as further described in §§ 1502.11 through 1502.18, in any appropriate format.

choice is unimportant. Sections with an asterisk (*) are usually retained in an EA; the others are omitted or combined with other sections.

 See *FCSG—Numbering Systems*

* Cover Sheet
   Summary
* Table of Contents
   Issue Tracking Matrix

*1.0	Purpose of and Need for Action
*2.0	Alternatives Including the Proposed Action
3.0	Affected Environment
*4.0	Environmental Consequences
5.0	List of Preparers
*6.0	List of Agencies, Organizations, and Persons to Whom Copies of the Statement Are Sent
	Index
A,B,C	Appendices (if any)

4. Some other information can appear as appendices or, if you wish, separately numbered chapters:

     Scoping Information

     Bibliography

     Glossary

     Maps

5. The comment letters on a Draft EIS are usually in a separate volume or, at the least, a separate chapter. As section 1503.4 of the CEQ Regulations explains, you must substantively respond to **all** comments, whether or not they require changes or adjustments to the EIS. See Response to Comments section (pp. 68–69).

6. Develop, as in example 6, a page layout (style sheet) for the EIS/EA. This layout should include the number of columns,

the size and nature of headings, the format for graphics, and page headers (or footers).

 See *FCSG—Page Layout*, for a sample style sheet. See also the entry on *Emphasis*.

Decisions about page layout require a decision about whether to number sections and subsections. Many early EISs used a standard outline numbering system: I, A, 1, a, etc. More recently, EISs are relying on different type styles and sizes to differentiate headings.

 See *FCSG—Numbering Systems*

2.0 Chapter Title

2.1 First-Level Heading

_____
_____

2.1.1 Second-Level Heading

_____
_____
_____

Third-Level Heading _____
_____
_____
_____

+-----------------------------+
| |
| |
| Graphic |
| |
| |
+-----------------------------+

Great Neck Bridge EIS   2–11

***EXAMPLE 6**—An established page layout helps all contributors to an EIS or EA to provide consistently written sections. NOTE: All examples are numbered to correspond to a suggestion for writing; they are not numbered consecutively.*

7. As early as possible, the interdisciplinary team (or writer/editor) should lay out the content and organization for everyone to use. As in example 7, a page-by-page mockup is an efficient way to lay out the content and make assignments.

Some people use a computer for mockups. Others prefer three-ring binders. Still others use an available wall.

Mock up on a computer. Computer mockups are becoming more and more common. Desktop publishing software and most word processing software allow you to design pages, set margins, and preview page layouts before you write a lot of text.

Begin your computer mockup with a rough page array (often with tentative headings or key words to remind you of each page's content). Spacing at this early stage will be inaccurate. Be sure to add text and insert rough visuals. If you've done a thorough job planning and discovering the details, you will already have a good deal of text finished.

Don't neglect to use a hard copy of the computer mockup as a reviewing tool for the decisionmaker and other resource specialists. They can easily begin to visualize the EIS or EA.

Include as many of the following features as you can in your mockup:

- Headings

- Lists

- Numbering systems

- Repetition

- White space

- Indentation

- Rules

- Boxes

- Visual aids

Mock up in three-ring binders. Begin with a binder filled with blank pages. As you plan, brainstorm, and organize, keep fleshing out the binder.

Mock up on a wall. For some EISs/EAs, consider filling a wall with pages from a complete chapter or section of an EIS or EA. Use either actual 8 1/2-by-11 sheets or flip chart pages. You and others can easily see where gaps are and then can move things around as appropriate.

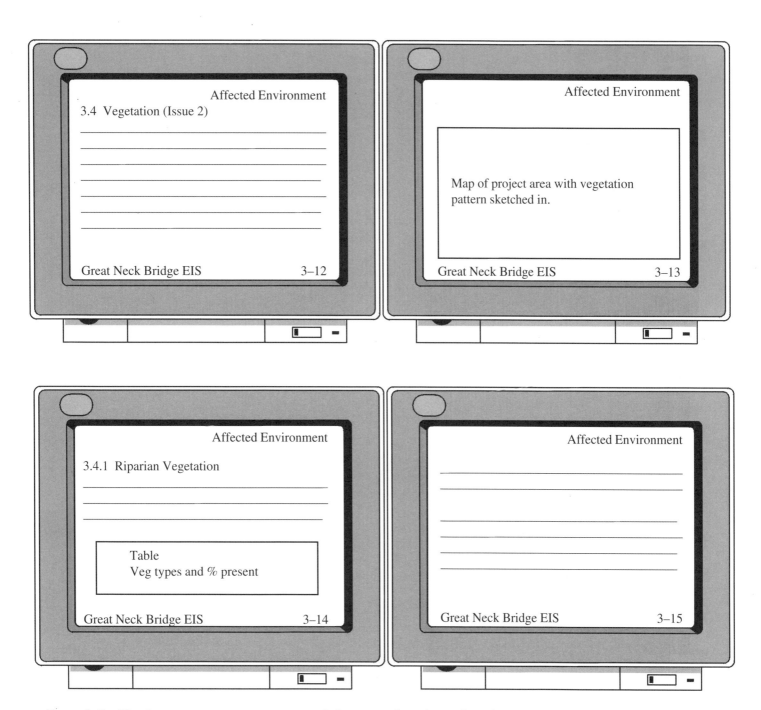

Example 7—*The above computer screens present only four pages from the mockup of an EIS. Develop a page-by-page mockup before you begin writing text. Use the mockup as a project management tool.*

COVER SHEET

SUGGESTIONS FOR WRITING

Cover Sheet

1. Include the name, title, and address of the responsible official (decisionmaker). See example 1 on the following page.

2. An abstract is likely unnecessary for most EAs. If included, the abstract should be as informative as possible but still brief.

 See *FCSG—Summaries*

As a minimum, include the following project-specific information in the abstract:

a. Explain **who** wants to do **what** and **where** and **why** they want to do it.
b. List the alternatives.
c. Identify the preferred alternative.

3. Add a *How to Read this EIS/EA* to the back of the Cover Sheet or perhaps in a separate card that can serve as a bookmark for the document. This guide should tell readers that Chapters 1 and 2 are an executive summary and that Chapters 3 and 4 contain supporting information. As appropriate, refer readers to special pages in the EIS/EA (for example, the Chapter 2 matrix that compares the effects of the alternatives). If you choose the card option, consider placing either a list of alternatives or a glossary of key terms on the back of the card.

CEQ REGULATIONS

§ 1502.11 Cover sheet.

The cover sheet shall not exceed one page. It shall include:

(a) A list of the responsible agencies including the lead agency and any cooperating agencies.
(b) The title of the proposed action that is the subject of the statement (and if appropriate the titles of related cooperating agency actions), together with the State(s) and county(ies) (or other jurisdiction if applicable) where the action is located.
(c) The name, address, and telephone number of the person at the agency who can supply further information.
(d) A designation of the statement as a draft, final, or draft or final supplement.
(e) A one paragraph abstract of the statement.
(f) The date by which comments must be received (computed in cooperation with EPA under § 1506.10).

The information required by this section may be entered on Standard Form 424 (in items 4, 6, 7, 10, and 18).

Cover Sheet

Proposed action:	SJCC (South Junction Coal Company) proposes to mine about 2.0 million tons of coal at its Salt Flat mine during the next 32 years.
Type of statement:	Final EIS (Environmental Impact Statement)
Lead agency:	OSM (Office of Surface Mining) Reclamation and Enforcement
Cooperating agencies:	Federal: 　Bureau of Indian Affairs 　BLM (Bureau of Land Management) State of New Mexico: 　Mining and Minerals Division
For further information:	Josephine Jacobs 　Attn: Charles Hawkins Office of Surface Mining Reclamation and Enforcement Brooks Towers 1020 - 15th Street Denver, Colorado 80202 (303) 844-xxxx (commercial) 564-xxxx (FTS)
Abstract:	SJCC (South Junction Coal Company) proposes to mine an average of about 2.0 million tons per year, or 69.7 million tons of coal over 32 years, at its Salt Flat mine. Production of coal would peak at 4.0 million tons per year after approximately 20 years of mining. Coal production would remain at 4.0 million tons per year for 3 years, then gradually decline over the remaining life of the mine. In the process, 1,551 acres of land would be disturbed on the mine area, the facilities area, and the transportation corridor addressed by SJCC's permit application package. An additional 92 acres would be disturbed during construction of that part of the transportation corridor within the permit area of the San Juan mine. Total disturbance, therefore, would be 1,643 acres. OSM and BLM have chosen as the preferred alternative to approve SJCC's mining and transportation plans. The EIS also assesses the potential impacts of five alternative transportation scenarios that were proposed by SJCC in response to public comment on the proposed southern coal haul road. The South Fork and Dry Run mines are in operation in the general area. The proposed Salt Flat mine, in conjunction with these other mines and other economic development projects, would moderately impact the social and economic conditions of Center City and of Jasper County, New Mexico. Impact of increased traffic on State Highway 140 from the operation would be significant. In addition, activities at the proposed mine and within the proposed transportation corridor would significantly impact two grazing permits. Other impacts would be moderate or negligible.

EXAMPLE 1—*This cover sheet, based on an Office of Surface Mining EIS, contains the essential information. Note that the abstract identifies the preferred alternative.*

SUMMARY

SUGGESTED CONTENT

The summary is a miniature EIS.

A. Purpose of and Need for Action (Chapter 1.0)
B. Alternatives Including the Proposed Action (Chapter 2.0)
C. Affected Environment (Chapter 3.0)
D. Environmental Consequences (Chapter 4.0)

NOTE: The organization parallels in miniature the recommended format of an EIS/EA. If necessary (and appropriate), add other information and headings.

SUGGESTIONS FOR WRITING

Summary (Optional for EA)

1. For EAs that can support a FONSI, replace the Summary with a well-written, stand-alone FONSI (combined with an EA decision document).

2. All of the essential information that is contained in the EIS should be in the Summary; repetition of information is inevitable.

 See *FCSG—Summaries*

We recommend organizing the summary by using section headings that parallel the main chapter headings in your EIS.

3. Whatever section headings you choose for the summary, include the following information:

- Explain **who** wants to do **what** and **where** and **why** they want to do it.

- Explain the decision(s) that the responsible official(s) must make.

- Identify the preferred alternative. Do not present the rationale for this alternative being preferred.

- Describe the potential major impacts (environmental consequences) if the preferred alternative were implemented.

- Briefly identify the alternatives that were considered.

- Discuss the areas of controversy. Make sure you accurately summarize the issues that are in the EIS.

4. If you know that the summary will be distributed separately, write a detailed 10- to 15-page summary and include appropriate graphics, such as a map and a matrix that compares the effects of the alternatives. These graphics may be duplicates of ones in the EIS/EA.

    If it will not be distributed separately, keep the summary short (3 to 5 pages).

5. Use graphics, an open format, and other techniques to make the summary highly readable. Many readers will read only the summary.

 See *FCSG—Graphics for Documents*

CEQ REGULATIONS

§ 1502.12 Summary.

Each environmental impact statement shall contain a summary which adequately and accurately summarizes the statement. The summary shall stress the major conclusions, areas of controversy (including issues raised by agencies and the public), and the issues to be resolved (including the choice among alternatives). The summary will normally not exceed 15 pages.

TABLE OF CONTENTS

SUGGESTIONS FOR WRITING

Table of Contents

1. Simplify "Table of Contents" to "Contents," as illustrated in Example 4, which is the first page from an actual contents page for a document. We retain the full (if somewhat wordy) title on these pages because CEQ Regulations uses the full title in list of recommended format items (Section 1502.10).

2. Include first-level subsections in your table of contents so that readers can accurately locate content within the various chapters. Always include second-level or even third-level headings, especially if you are writing a complex, long EIS.

CEQ REGULATIONS

Table of contents.

No CEQ Regulations exist for this section, even though it is part of the document.

THIS	4.4.3 Direct Effects on Water Quality
	or
	4.4.3 Direct Effects (Water Quality Issue)
NOT THIS	4.4.3 Direct Effects

EXAMPLE 3—*Substantive headings help readers skim and scan for key points. Good headings tell a story.*

 See *FCSG—Tables of Content*

3. Here and elsewhere in the EIS/EA, use headings that help readers keep track of where they are. As in example 3, add clarifying words or phrases throughout.

4. As in example 4, you may number headings and subheadings. Many early EISs used a standard outline numbering system: I, A, 1, a, etc. Others used a scientific system: 1.0, 1.1, 1.1.1, 1.1.2, etc. More recently, EISs are relying on different type styles and sizes to differentiate lower-level headings.

See *FCSG—Numbering Systems*

We recommend retaining numbers for the chapters and the next level of headings. Lower level headings need not be numbered.

5. Number the pages of your preliminary materials (such as the table of contents and the summary) with small Roman numerals: i, ii, etc. As an option, you could number the summary in this manner: S–1, S–2, etc.

6. Number your pages either sequentially from the beginning of the document to the end or chapter by chapter (3–5, 3–6, etc.) with the chapter number coming before the en dash. An en dash is longer than a hyphen, but shorter than a normal dash (called an em dash).

7. Number appendices by using the appendix letter (or number) along with a page number: A–1, A–2, etc.

8. As a supplement to a table of contents, consider including a matrix displaying how each chapter (section) of the EIS responds to the significant issues. See example 8.

   If you decide to include this matrix, place it either following the table of contents or at the end of the EIS/EA (on a foldout sheet).

  FCSG—Tables of Contents

Contents

	List of Tables	iii
	List of Figures	v
	Issue Tracking Matrix	vi
	Summary	ix
Chapter 1.0	Purpose of and Need for Action	
	1.1 Introduction	1
	1.2 Decision Needed	2
	1.3 Scoping Summary	3
	1.4 Relevant Issues	4
	1.5 Summary of Prior Legal Action	8
Chapter 2.0	Alternatives Including the Proposed Action	
	2.1 Alternatives Considered	11
	2.2 Range of Alternatives and Alternatives Eliminated	13
	2.3 Summary of the Environmental Effects of Alternatives	23
	2.4 Identification of the Agency Preferred Alternative	22

EXAMPLE **4**—*Always include second-level headings in your contents. Third- or fourth-level headings are optional, but they would help your readers visualize the whole EIS or EA.*

Issue Tracking Matrix

ISSUES	Summary	1.0 Purpose and Need	2.0 Alternatives	3.0 Affected Environment	4.0 Environmental Consequences	Appendix A Public Involvement	Appendix B
1. Soil Stability	2	6–7	12, 14–15	22–25	61–65, 81	A–3, A–5	B–6, B–11, and B–15
2. Water Quality	2–3	7	12, 15–16	26–30	66–70, 81–84	A–3, A–5	B–5, B–8, and B–20
3. Wildlife	3	7–8	12, 17	33–37	73, 78, 84–85	A–5, A–14, A–20, and A–24	B–13 and B–22
OBJECTIVES							
1. Maintenance Area (sq.ft.)	4–5	8	12, 18	38–41	85-86, 92	A–5, A–15, and A–24	B–22 and B–24
2. Construction Costs ($)	5	8	12, 18	42–45	87–88, 91	A–5 and A–23	B–23 and B–24
3. Two-Way Access	5	9–10	12, 19	46–49	89–90, 92	A–15 and A–16	B–22 and B–24

EXAMPLE **8**—*An issue tracking matrix tells readers you have covered each issue thoroughly and consistently.*

Purpose of and Need for Action (Chapter 1.0)

§ 1502.13 Purpose and need.

The statement shall briefly specify the underlying purpose and need to which the agency is responding in proposing the alternatives including the proposed action.

Suggested Content

Sections with an asterisk (*) are usually retained in an EA; the others are omitted or combined with other sections.

*1.0 Purpose of and Need for Action

Make your purpose and need an honest, full explanation of why the agency is considering an action and what the agency objectives are.

    *1.1 Explain **who** wants to do **what** and **where** and **why** they want to do it. Include project objectives.

    *1.2 Explain any other EISs/EAs that influence the scope of this EIS/EA.

    *1.3 Explain the decision(s) that must be made and identify any other agencies involved in this NEPA analysis.

    *1.4 Summarize the scoping and explain the relevant issues. As appropriate, identify issues considered but discarded from detailed analysis.

    *1.5 List Federal permits, licenses, entitlements necessary to implement the project.

    1.6 Preview the remaining chapters of your EIS/EA, especially if you have changed the CEQ organization.

Suggestions for Writing

*1.0 Purpose of and Need for Action

Note: Use the full heading as given in section 1502.10 for this chapter: Purpose of and Need for Action. Sometimes, this CEQ heading is combined with the word *Introduction*—for example, "Introduction: Purpose of and Need for Action".

    *1.1 Explain <u>who</u> wants to do <u>what</u> and <u>where</u> and <u>why</u> they want to do it. Include project objectives.

1.1.1 Open with a brief summary of the proposed action. This statement sets up the following detailed explanation of the purpose and need for both the proposed action and the other alternatives. See example 1.1.1.

1.1.2 Explain the purpose and need for the action in terms of the person or agency that is proposing the action. Begin by explaining the on-the-ground purpose and need, **not** the NEPA requirement to write an EIS or EA. (A sentence or two about the NEPA requirements can follow this opening discussion of purpose and need.)

1.1.3 Objectives are especially important to this initial discussion of purpose and need. Objectives arise from many sources: a law, agency mission, a prior NEPA document, or another agency's objective (perhaps based on a state law).

As you write either an EIS or EA, list the objectives, give their source, and give measurement indicators, as illustrated in Example 1.1.3. As appropriate, tell readers just how firm or binding an objective must be. For instance, a Federal law authorizing a water supply project might set an objective dealing with salmon spawning (say 50 percent annual increase by the end of the decade). This objective is a fixed target, although even in this instance an agency might find that the 50 percent increase is impossible. Or an even clearer example, if state water quality standards specify a maximum amount of sediment in a stream, then all legal NEPA alternatives would need to achieve this standard.

Finally, avoid listing as objectives the project actions that you are proposing. For instance, an improper objective would be to build a 3-mile extension to county road 23A. The actual objective would possibly be the need to provide year-round access to a stream monitoring station. In this case, maybe a road is unnecessary because a helicopter would be more environmentally desirable. A sound objective usually allows different options or alternatives as ways to achieve the objective.

1.1.4 Objectives are also important because they help an agency to define the minimum standards that the proposed action and alternatives must meet. Conceptually, these standards, sometimes called selection criteria, help the agency define the range of reasonable alternatives it will analyze in the EIS or EA.

As an example, consider a proposed project dealing with a new vehicle maintenance facility. The agency proposing such a project surveys its current fleet of vehicles, analyzes maintenance records, and projects the number of additional vehicles to be added to the fleet. Based on this data, the agency estimates that it needs at least eight repair bays or a minimum floor space of 5,500 square feet.

This estimate of needed floor space becomes a minimum standard, and all alternatives analyzed should include floor space of about 5,500 square feet. An alternative that allocated only 3,500 square feet would not be a reasonable alternative.

See the discussion in section 2.1.2 (p. 26) for additional information about minimum standards.

1.1.5 Include a location map to show **where** the action would take place if it were implemented. Be sure to prepare a location map that is tailored to the specific EIS/EA, not one from your map file.

 See *FCSG—Maps*

The Department of Energy proposes to upgrade in fiscal year 1994 its security at the Atlas facility by adding a 30-foot guard tower at the eastern entrance and replacing the outdated electronic sensor system currently installed in the perimeter fence.

Example 1.1.1—*The lead sentence in 1.0 is actually a brief summary of the proposed action.*

Project Objectives (Measurement Indicators, if possible)

- Allow for improved access in case of fires (Land Management Plan, p. 4–18). (Miles of road available)

- Protect golden trout habitat (LMP, p. 4–34, and State Fish and Game objective—Letter 10/25/90). (Miles of streamside habitat)

- Reduce erosion caused by ORVs (ORV EA, p. 17). (Sediment)

- Provide storage space for munitions for 14 A-10 aircraft. (Square feet of storage space)

Example 1.1.3—*Project objectives (also called goals or the mission) are key starting points in any NEPA analysis.*

*1.2 Introduce and explain how related EISs, EAs, and other documents influence the scope of this EIS/EA.

1.2.1 Explain the linkage (tiering) between any prior EIS/EA and the EIS/EA you are working on. See sections 1502.20 and 1508.28 of the CEQ Regulations for a general explanation of tiering. Note here and repeat in Chapter 2 any indication that one or more alternatives may not be consistent with this prior EIS/EA.

Management decisions about scope should be clear from the first to the interdisciplinary team. Written guidance is a valuable management tool.

1.2.2 Tiering is not a brief reference to another NEPA document. As in example 1.2.2, establish the specific links between the two NEPA documents. For example, if the prior EIS/EA allocated land to grazing, that decision quite properly limits the scope of your proposed action to grazing, not recreational improvements. Be prepared to cite specific guidance.

*1.3 Explain the decision(s) that must be made and identify any other agencies involved in this NEPA analysis.

1.3.1 The decision(s) to be made are directly connected to the scope of the actions (and ultimately, the alternatives and potential impacts). See section 1508.25 of the CEQ Regulations.

For example, management often has the option of proposing an action in a given fiscal year, such as the development of a hiking trail. Such a proposal is contingent on public need, agency budgets, and prior NEPA planning. As early as possible, the decisionmaker needs to establish the scope for this

proposed action. Will the trail system extend beyond the Cattle Creek drainage? Should a trailhead parking lot be part of the proposed action? These up-front decisions on scope should appear in a project initiation memo to the interdisciplinary team.

More important, the scope of the decisions to be made must be carefully explained in this section of Chapter 1. See example 1.3.1.

1.3.2 When the proposed action originates outside the agency, as in a mining request or a summer home permit, the agency's decision space is especially important.

1.3.3 Sometimes part of the decision might already have been made and recorded in a previous land-use EIS. For example, in a timber sale on a national forest, the responsible official might already have approved an area for a timber sale. The decision in an EA would then focus on when and how to harvest.

*1.4 Summarize the scoping and explain the relevant issues. As appropriate, identify issues considered but discarded from detailed analysis.

1.4.1 Summarize scoping because scoping is a critical NEPA activity (see section 1501.7 of the CEQ Regulations). Remember that a full record of all scoping activities is properly part of the background documentation for the EIS/EA—in either an appendix or in the analysis file. See the discussion of the Analysis File (Planning Record) on pp. 81–84.

According to the Goat Creek Planning EIS, land on the north side of Summit Ridge provides moderate quality grazing for three existing allotments. According to the EIS (p. 145), improved grazing is a goal, contingent on changes in grazing intensity and some seasonal restrictions. The present EA will address these changes in its alternatives.

Example 1.2.2—*Tiering requires careful page references to the prior NEPA document.*

---

a. To deny the permit (no action)
b. To approve the permit as submitted
c. To approve the permit with specific management constraints and mitigation measures

Example 1.3.1—*The decisionmaker's options are important guides as to the possible scope of the alternatives to be analyzed.*

Most Federal agencies have routinely introduced scoping in Chapter 1, and most readers now expect to see a list of significant issues in Chapter 1.

A few agencies prefer to introduce scoping and the relevant issues in Chapter 2. This variation in organization is not important as long as either Chapter 1 or Chapter 2 contains a list of relevant issues.

1.4.2 Mention your efforts to involve other agencies and members of the public. Specifically reference either your appendix on scoping or your analysis file so that all scoping information becomes part of the legal record.

1.4.3 Identify the "significant issues" (see sections 1500.4 and 1501.7 of the CEQ Regulations). This use of "significant" is confusing because the term has a second and different legal meaning, as reflected in the Finding of No Significant Impact. Given this confusion, we recommend that writers of EISs and EAs choose another term, such as "relevant," to label those issues that are important to their NEPA analysis. Note that the impacts of such relevant or major issues are not always significant in the legal sense even in EISs. And in EAs, the impacts will never be significant unless the agency has discovered or is in the process of discovering that it needs to prepare an EIS, not an EA. See the decision tree in example 1.4.3 for a conceptualization of how to determine which issues are relevant.

An issue is an effect (or a perceived effect, risk, or hazard) on a physical, biological, social, or economic resource. An issue is **not** an activity; instead, the predicted effects of the activity create the issue. CEQ Regulations indicate that agencies are responsible for a clear and efficient definition of issues.

How to Decide If an Issue Is Relevant (That Is, Significant, As Directed by the CEQ Regulations)

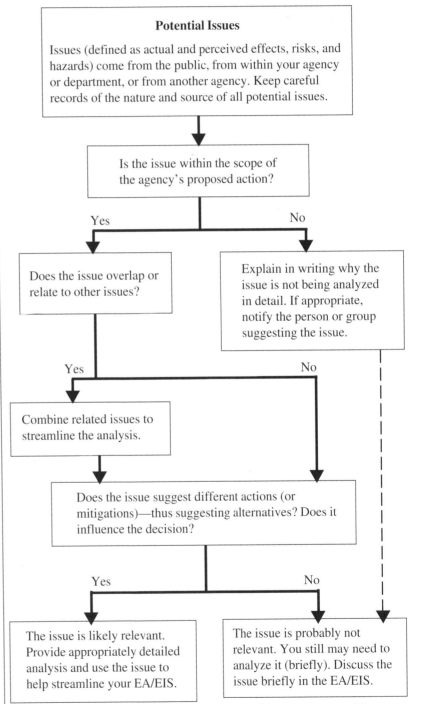

EXAMPLE 1.4.3—*Issues can arise at any time and from any source. The Federal department or agency must carefully analyze and prioritize all potential issues.*

The interdisciplinary team may begin the analysis with two dozen potentially relevant issues. Only those that turn out to be relevant should appear in this chapter.

1.4.4 Frame your relevant issues by mentioning, first, the action or actions that will cause potential effects. Next, explain how different potential effects relate to each other. Your goal is to educate readers as to why a particular issue is truly relevant (and, thus, important to the decision at hand).

See examples 1.4.4–1 and 1.4.4–2 for ways to write up your issues. Other write-ups might begin with a question: "What will be the impacts on bighorn sheep?" Whatever approach you use, give readers enough information so that they can see why each issue is relevant to the scope of the action and the decisions needed. Cite backup data and technical reports as necessary.

ISSUES FROM THE BELTRANE MINING EIS

A.   **Impacts on the bighorn sheep**

- Beltrane Mining vehicles might disturb bighorn sheep, causing them to move away from Road 28N to areas of less favorable habitat. Such a displacement could change the ratio of rams to ewes, which is a reflection of the viability of a population.
  Indicator: ram/ewe ratios (%).

- Vehicular disturbance to bighorn sheep would be probable near the mineral lick and lambing area that adjoin Road 28N. This lambing area is one of five known for the sheep using the Sweet Canyon area (figure 3, p. 5). Disturbance close to the lambing area might affect the number of lambs surviving to adulthood.
  Indicator: lamb survival (%).

- A decline in bighorn sheep near Road 28N would decrease existing recreational and educational opportunities to view and to study the sheep.
  Indicator: RVDs (Recreation Visitor Days).

B.   **Increased erosion as well as a decrease in water quality because of either the heavy maintenance of Road 31S or the reconstruction of Road 31S**

- Erosion might add sediment to the Big Muddy channel and perhaps contribute to the silting of the Lucas Reservoir.
  Indicator: sediment.

- Aquatic organisms and fisheries in the Big Muddy and in the Lucas Reservoir probably would be harmed by a decline in water quality.
  Indicator: number of catch or fish and their reproductive success rates.

- Water from the Big Muddy ultimately flows into Lucas Reservoir and then into Eastgate Reservoir, which is a source of municipal water. Removal of added sediment would increase the cost of water purification.
  Indicator: cost ($).

EXAMPLE 1.4.4–1—*Issues arise when the agency (or another interested party) identifies an effect that they would like to avoid or mitigate. Use the issue statements to educate readers about what the problems and choices are.*

1.4.5 Mention what indicators (quantifications) you propose to use to measure the environmental consequences. In example 1.4.4–1, both the ram/ewe ratio and the annual survival rate of lambs would be key measures (indicators) of the effects on bighorn sheep in the project area.

As part of your write-up of the issue, you should list such indicators:

Indicators (Standards)
—Ram/ewe ratios
—Annual lamb survival

ISSUES FROM THE BIG MEADOW GRAZING EA

Issue 1. Composition of Vegetation (Biodiversity)

Cattle grazing could weaken or even kill the native grasses, which currently constitute about 50 percent of the vegetation in Big Meadow.

Range analysis in 1976 and 1989 on an adjacent and similar range area shows that weedy herbaceous plants often replaced weakened and dying native grasses (Grazing Report in Appendix C). This decline in native grasses would permanently change in the natural biodiversity of the high meadow plant community (Pearson, A. L., pp. 74–75). This shift in vegetative composition could permanently decrease the usable and nutritious forage, either for livestock or for elk. (See issue 3 below.)

Indicator: Potential effects of the different alternatives will be estimated in light of the ratio of native grasses to weedy herbaceous plants.

Issue 2. Soil Erosion and Meadow Productivity

Some of the areas where grass could die have soil that is a highly erodible, silty loam (Soil Conservation Service, 1975). If exposed, this loam could erode, forming rills and gullies during heavy summer rainstorms. Any loss of surface soils would further impair the ability of Big Meadow to produce vegetation, particularly grass.

Indicator: Potential effects of the soil loss would be estimated in light of the number of acres likely to be subject to erosion. This acreage would be an indirect indication of the vegetative productivity.

Issue 3. Elk Grazing vs. Cattle Grazing

Decreased grass and lower vegetative productivity would have an effect on the elk that historically graze on Big Meadow primarily from July through October. Data from the Department of Natural Resources (Utah Department of Natural Resources, 1987), suggest that elk from the Unit 22 herd are relying on Big Meadow forage to carry them into the fall breeding season and into the often harsh winters.

Indicator: The estimated number of elk using Big Meadow constitute current grazing use, as measured in AUMs (Animal Use Months). Cattle grazing would consume additional AUMs and could deprive elk of necessary grazing.

EXAMPLE **1.4.4–2**—*Well-written, accurate issues educate readers about the potential effects of the proposed action and alternatives.*

Establish that you have made a good-faith effort to deal with all potential issues.

See the discussion of the analysis file on pp. 81–84.

1.4.6 As appropriate, list and explain any issues discussed but considered not relevant for the purposes of your analysis. Often you need only refer readers to your scoping appendix (or analysis file), especially if suggested issues have been numerous. The requirement is that everyone's suggested issue has been fairly and clearly dealt with and that you have provided a clear paper trail as part of your legal record.

*1.5   List Federal permits, licenses, entitlements necessary to implement the project.

1.5.1 Specify who is responsible for obtaining the different permits. Often, as in mining projects, the person responsible will be the miner. At times, however, the agency will need to obtain a permit or a license.

1.5.2 In some cases, different alternatives may require different permits. Be sure to explain such differences either here or when you describe the alternatives in Chapter 2.

One such difference might be the need to amend an existing land management plan if a certain alternative is selected.

1.5.3 List, if appropriate, any state or local permits. For example, states have permit authority over water quality issues.

1.6   Preview the remaining chapters of your EIS/EA, especially if you have changed the CEQ organization.

1.6.1 This preview is unnecessary for most EAs, unless you have decided to change the CEQ organization.

1.6.2 Some editors would prefer not to place this preview at the end of Chapter 1. As an option, these editors would prefer to write what is often called a preface telling readers how best to approach the content chapters that follow. This preface would usually follow the contents and would be numbered with lowercase Roman numerals.

Other editors have chosen to include such information on a summary card that readers can use as a bookmark; in such cases, the card usually lists alternatives on one side, with guidance for readers on the other side.

ALTERNATIVES INCLUDING THE PROPOSED ACTION (CHAPTER 2.0)

SUGGESTED CONTENT

Sections with an asterisk (*) are usually retained in an EA; the others are omitted or combined with other sections.

*2.0 **Alternatives Including the Proposed Action**

    *2.1 Explain that this chapter describes the alternatives (potential actions). Also remind readers that this chapter summarizes the environmental consequences of the alternatives.

    *2.2 Describe the alternatives, including the proposed action and no action. Your descriptions should focus on potential actions, outputs, and any related mitigations.

    2.3 Explain how these alternatives represent a range of reasonable alternatives. As part of this explanation, describe briefly the alternatives eliminated from detailed study and explain why they were eliminated.

    *2.4 Compare the alternatives by summarizing their environmental consequences and, as appropriate, their achievement of objectives. Potential actions and outputs would cause these consequences.

    2.5 Identify your agency's preferred alternative, unless your agency directs otherwise. Do not give in the EIS/EA the rationale for your choice. Include the rationale in the ROD or Decision Document/ FONSI.

SUGGESTIONS FOR WRITING

*2.0 **Alternatives Including the Proposed Action**

    *2.1 **Explain that this chapter both describes the alternatives (potential actions) and summarizes the environmental consequences of the alternatives.**

2.1.1 Remind readers that this chapter does more than merely describe the alternatives. As the CEQ guidance in section 1502.14 emphasizes, the heart of this chapter is to sharply define the differences between the alternatives, especially in how their environmental impacts differ.

CEQ REGULATIONS

§ 1502.14 Alternatives including the proposed action.

This section is the heart of the environmental impact statement. Based on the information and analysis presented in the sections on the Affected Environment (§ 1502.15) and the Environmental Consequences (§ 1502.16), it should present the environmental impacts of the proposal and the alternatives in comparative form, thus sharply defining the issues and providing a clear basis for choice among options by the decisionmaker and the public. In this section agencies shall:

(a) Rigorously explore and objectively evaluate all reasonable alternatives, and for alternatives which were eliminated from detailed study, briefly discuss the reasons for their having been eliminated.

(b) Devote substantial treatment to each alternative considered in detail including the proposed action so that reviewers may evaluate their comparative merits.

(c) Include reasonable alternatives not within the jurisdiction of the lead agency.

(d) Include the alternative of no action.

(e) Identify the agency's preferred alternative or alternatives, if one or more exists, in the draft statement and identify such alternative in the final statement unless another law prohibits the expression of such a preference.

(f) Include appropriate mitigation measures not already included in the proposed action or alternatives.

2.1.2 Review for readers the conceptual linkage between the purpose and need (including project objectives), as introduced in Chapter 1, the relevant (significant) environmental issues, also introduced in Chapter 1, and the range of reasonable alternatives to be presented in Chapter 2.

A reasonable alternative is one that achieves, in large part, the agency's defined purpose and need while not violating any minimum environmental standards, as introduced in the discussion of relevant environmental issues.

As an example, assume that an agency is proposing to provide additional parking space for visitors to a recreational site. Current usage patterns show that the existing lot is always full during the peak summer season and that vehicles waiting for parking space clog the nearby access roads. The agency estimates that a new or expanded lot would require at least 400 parking spaces. This estimate is based on current use and a projected increase in use over the next decade. A relevant environmental issue is an existing wetlands that borders two sides of the current parking area.

A reasonable alternative for this proposed parking area would be one that provided at least 400 parking spaces (or close to that number) but did not damage the adjoining wetlands. An alternative that provided only 200 parking spaces (almost no change from the existing lot) would not be feasible. Similarly, an alternative that damaged the wetlands would not meet the minimum environmental standards established by the Executive Order on wetlands.

For more information about minimal standards or, as they are often called, selection criteria, see the discussion in section 1.1.4 (p. 19).

2.1.3 Refer to the interdisciplinary nature of the alternatives and to the role of the interdisciplinary approach throughout this critical step in the NEPA process.

2.1.4 In an EIS and in longer EAs (over 30 pages), list the content (headings) to follow, as in example 2.1.4.

*2.2 Describe the alternatives, including the proposed action and no action. Your descriptions should focus on potential actions, outputs, and any related mitigations.

2.2.1 Make your descriptions as site-specific as possible. Your goal is to show to the decisionmaker and readers exactly what would happen on the ground if a particular alternative were implemented. Unless you are site-specific in this EIS/EA, you run the risk of having to repeat the NEPA analysis and documentation.

Usually, information about an alternative is a mixture of potential actions and outputs. Typical actions would be constructing a road, cutting timber, installing a utility line, or allowing an outfitter guide to enter an area. Typical outputs would be 3.2 miles of new road, 10 million board feet of timber, 4 miles of 3-inch diameter underground conduit, and 15 visitor days per recreation area.

Often, actions and outputs can be summarized for all alternatives, as illustrated in example 2.2.1. Such a summary is different from the summary of environmental consequences.

 See *FCSG—Maps*

Use clear site-specific maps for each alternative, including no action. These maps are variations of the general location map you included in Chapter 1.

2.2 Description of Alternatives, Including the Proposed Action and No Action

2.3 Description of Alternatives Considered but Eliminated from Detailed Study

2.4 A Comparison of Environmental Consequences

2.5 Identification of the Preferred Alternative (optional for an EA)

EXAMPLE 2.1.4—*A preview of contents should appear in every chapter. As an option, print the major subheads on the divider page before the chapter begins.*

Alternative	Acres Disturbed	Miles of Road	Seasonal Closure
A (No Action)	0	0	All Year
B	125	2.7	April 1 to June 15
C	140	3.4	April 1 to June 1

EXAMPLE 2.2.1—*The list of activities and outputs will replace hard-to-read text.*

*Management
requirements,
mitigations, and
monitoring reflect
different ways of
responding to the
relevant issues.*

2.2.2 Include management requirements, mitigations, and monitoring in your description of each alternative. These details will help you flesh out for readers exactly what would happen on the ground if an alternative were implemented.

As in example 2.2.2, some management requirements and monitoring may be specific to a single alternative.

2.2.3 Consolidate management requirements, monitoring, or mitigations into a single list if they are common to every action alternative. Place this list either at the beginning or the end of this section of Chapter 2. If such a list is quite extensive, you might want to include it in an appendix and reference it in this section of Chapter 2.

Make this consolidated list as complete as possible so that during implementation no item will be overlooked. Include, if available, the person responsible for each action and the approximate timing of the action.

2.2.4 Define for readers both the proposed action and the no action alternative.

The proposed action is, usually, what the agency (or decisionmaker) is thinking about doing when the NEPA analysis begins. As such, it may or may not be what the decisionmaker finally chooses to implement. In some EISs/EAs no proposed action appears; instead, the agency merely addresses alternative ways to achieve objectives and to manage the resources.

No action has two common meanings: (1) Continue present management activities, but do not do the proposed project (or defer the proposed action), and (2) don't do anything. See example 2.2.4 for a sample writeup of a no action alternative. Tell readers which meaning of *no action* you are using. Always analyze and fully discuss the no action alternative. Also, remind readers that the no action alternative is the baseline for all the rest of your analysis. Under no action, environmental consequences will still occur because the existing environment is not static.

Alternative 3

Alternative 3 would increase the AUMs to 1,811. It would use a three-pasture rest-rotation grazing system. Under this alternative, the permittee would be required to transport the cattle by truck between the winter range and the mountain summer range. The permittee would be required to keep the fences in sound condition at his own expense.

Management Requirements

The Pearl Gate would be closed to public access during the elk calving season. The State Fish and Game would ensure that gates are secure.

All fences would be upgraded to four strands of barbed wire within 3 years by the permittee.

Monitoring Requirements

The FWS (Fish and Wildlife Service) would check the condition of the pastures several times during the spring, summer, and fall months.

The permittee is required to monitor the conditions of the pastures regularly and to report problems to the FWS if they occur.

EXAMPLE 2.2.2—*Each alternative description should contain all potential action and restrictions. The EIS (or EA) can then present the effects of the entire alternative.*

2.2.5 Make Alternative A (or Alternative 1) no action. Making no action the first listed alternative will usually help readers track the impacts of later action alternatives because no action is the conceptual baseline for these impacts. Not all agencies and their editors agree with this recommendation, and CEQ Regulations do not specify how to number and arrange alterantives.

2.2.6 Describe each alternative as it *would be*. Do not use *will.*

Alternative A **would manage** for a "pristine-primitive" environment. It **would emphasize** near natural conditions. All man-made "improvements" **would be removed**.

2.2.7 Use short titles for your alternatives if possible. These titles often can be the key action or output: *3.5 miles of road* or *4.5 million board feet.* They rarely will be more general phrases such as *wildlife alternative* or *commodity alternative* because such general labels too clearly distort the nature of the multiple actions within each alternative.

2.2.8 As part of tiering, identify any of the alternatives that are not consistent with a prior EIS/EA for the project area. Note that the interdisciplinary team properly should consider such alternatives because the environmental conditions (and issues) may have changed since the prior EIS/EA was prepared. Analyzing such alternatives gives the decisionmaker the latitude to choose one of these alternatives and, thus, to amend the prior NEPA decision.

2.2.9 Include and analyze reasonable alternatives outside the jurisdiction of your agency. Some reasonable alternatives might be illegal now but could become legal later because of your recommendation.

Alternative A: Continue Present Access, Maintenance, and Use (No Action)

Under No Action, the Bureau of Reclamation would neither improve nor restrict access to Reclamation land in the Yellowtooth Basin. The current situation as described below would continue. See Chapter III (Affected Environment) for a more detailed profile of the current environmental situation in the Basin.

Current access is by unimproved Reclamation road 2W112, much of which is in poor condition, especially after rain. Road 2W112 crosses a half mile of Ute tribal land and then fords Crystal Creek. Reclamation has no right-of-way to the segment controlled by the Ute Tribe. The ford at Crystal Creek is often impassable due to heavy spring runoff and summer thunderstorms.

Current uses include noncommercial post and pole firewood harvest (under Reclamation permits); some fishing and hunting, especially during elk season; and limited summer use by three small placer mines above the ford on Crystal Creek. This level of use is not expected to increase unless road 2W112 were improved, including some provision for an all-season crossing of Crystal Creek. Reclamation currently issues the firewood permits, and Reclamation has approved plans of operation for the miners, although nothing guarantees any of these users easy access or adequate maintenance of road 2W112.

Current maintenance is minimal. About every other year, Reclamation has sent a grader into the Yellowtooth Basin to smooth out ruts and repair washed out sections of road 2W112. Reclamation has provided limited gravel or fill. Total maintenance costs average about $2,500 for each time Reclamation has sent the grader in. The miners have also done some limited intermittent maintenance, with Reclamation approval.

Other access options include a proposed spur to the mining operations using private land. One miner has stated his intention to construct this short spur (roughly a quarter mile from the end of 2W112). If he completes the spur (likely gravel, low-standard construction), this road would provide a second access route to the Yellowtooth Basin, assuming the miner permitted public travel on the spur. This road would make 2W112 a loop route. This mining spur would become important if the Ute Tribe decided to deny access across their segment of existing 2W112.

EXAMPLE 2.2.4—*Under no action, things do occur—both naturally and as the result of agency or departmental management.*

Reasonable alternatives are those that are technically implementable, whether by your agency or by other agencies or private groups.

2.3 Explain how these alternatives represent a range of reasonable alternatives. As part of this explanation, describe briefly the alternatives eliminated from detailed study and explain why they were eliminated.

2.3.1 Review for readers the conceptual linkage between the purpose and need (including project objectives), as introduced in Chapter 1; the relevant (significant) environmental issues, also introduced in Chapter 1; and the range of reasonable alternatives presented in Chapter 2. A reasonable alternative is one that achieves, in large part, the agency's defined purpose and need while not violating any minimum environmental standards. See the discussions under sections 2.1.2 (pp. 26–27) and 1.1.4 (p. 19).

In some rare instances, an agency may analyze an alternative that is not feasible, perhaps because it is technically unrealistic or economically too costly. The agency's purpose in such instances is to show by detailed analysis that such an alternative is definitely not feasible.

2.3.2 Briefly discuss how the interdisciplinary team arrived at decisions about what constitutes reasonable alternatives. As part of this discussion, describe alternatives discarded during the analysis process. If necessary, provide detailed information in a separate appendix and be sure to retain documentation of such decisions in your analysis file (the legal record).

The four action alternatives all would harvest much the same volume of timber, but they differ in both where the harvest would be and how they would access the timber. Alternative A (No Action) would harvest no timber and would require no new roads. Alternative B would harvest 12.8 MMBF (million board feet) from units (areas) that are to the west of Forest Road 2N03. These units will require 3.1 miles of new road and 5.7 miles of road reconstruction. Alternative C would harvest 11.7 MMBF from units from both sides of 2N03. These units would require only 1.5 miles of new road and some 7.8 miles of road reconstruction. Alternative D . . .

EXAMPLE 2.3.3–1—*The range of activities available to an agency will depend on the site, the agency budget, the departmental mission, or other management goals. Always make these constraints clear.*

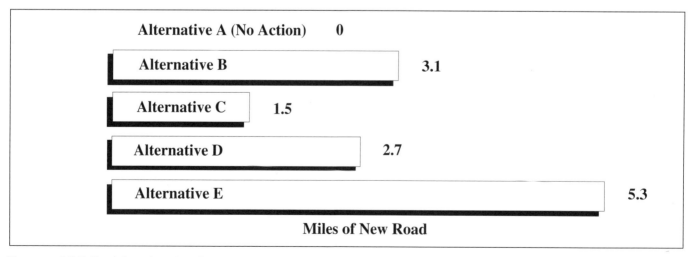

EXAMPLE 2.3.3–2—*A bar chart is only one way to present graphically that the alternatives contain different levels of action. As in this example, new road construction is only one of the project activities that might change from one alternative to another.*

2.3.3 A range of alternatives is a key legal requirement, so failing to describe the range in an EIS/EA can be a critical omission. As examples 2.3.3–1 and 2.3.3–2 indicate, you should explicitly explain how you are defining the range for your project.

2.3.4 Examples 2.3.3–1 and 2.3.3–2 focus on actions and outputs, but a second way to look at the range of alternatives is to consider how the alternatives differ in regard to their different types and degrees of effects. In example 2.3.3–1, even though the harvest level remains much the same in all alternatives, the effects might be very different based on the different units to be harvested and the different road systems.

*2.4 Compare the alternatives by summarizing their environmental consequences and, as appropriate, their achievement of objectives. Potential actions and outputs would cause these consequences.

2.4.1 The environmental consequences are the key to distinguishing between the alternatives, so make this section as readable and accessible as possible. Most agencies routinely build a comparative matrix into this section of Chapter 2. This matrix usually has the alternatives on one axis and the relevant issues and objectives on the other axis. For each issue and objective, the axis is usually further subdivided into indicators or measurements, as in examples 2.4.1–1 and 2.4.1–2.

Section 2.4 is a managerial summary of Chapter 4.

As appropriate, supplement the matrix with other graphics.

 See *FCSG— Graphics for Documents*

Table II-2: Project <u>Purpose and Need Indicators</u> and <u>Outputs</u>, Summary Comparison of Alternatives

Purpose and Need Indicators and Project Objectives	Alternative 1 No Action	Alternative 2 Proposed Action	Alternative 3	Alternative 4	Alternative 5
Forest Condition Indicators					
- Acres/percent commercially treated of <u>high priority</u> forest stands	0 acres 0% treated	4,000 ac. 65% treated	3,400 ac. 55% treated	1,950 ac. 31% treated	2,950 ac. 48% treated
- Acres/percent commercially treated of <u>moderate priority</u> forest stands	0 acres 0% treated	1,700 ac. 44% treated	1,400 ac. 36% treated	1,100 ac. 28% treated	1,200 ac. 31% treated
- Acres/percent treated of <u>overstocked</u> 10-30 year old tree plantations	0 acres 0% treated	2,580 ac. 79% treated	2,580 ac. 79% treated	2,255 ac. 69% treated	2,305 ac. 70% treated
- Acres underburned of Silviculture activity fuels	0 acres	7,285 ac.	6,790 ac.	5,220 ac.	6,160 ac.
- Acres underburned for natural fuels	0 acres	1,105 ac.	1,105 ac.	1,105 ac.	1,855 ac.
Wildlife Habitat Indicators					
- Acres underburned for big game forage	0 acres 0% treated	4,020 ac. 80% treated	4,020 ac. 80% treated	0 ac. 0% treated	0 ac. 0% treated
Watershed Indicators					
- Miles of roads decommissioned*	-	5.69	5.42	5.41	5.69
- Miles of roads closed	-	4.7	4.7	4.7	4.7
- Miles of roads reconstructed	-	13.5	13.5	13.5	13.5
Economic Indicators					
- Commercial Timber Volume (MMBF)		20	16	9	14
- Timber Market Value ($)		$2.3 mil	$1.9 mil	$1.3 mil	$2.0 mil
- Payment to Counties ($)		$584,000	$487,000	$335,000	$507,000

* Includes both System and Non-system Roads

EXAMPLE 2.4.1–1—*Table II-2 shows how the alternatives compare in terms of the Chapter 1 objectives. This table, with its achievement outputs, is the basis for the different environmental impacts presented in Tables II-3 and II-4.*

Figure-1: Stand Treatment Priority, Comparisons of Alternatives

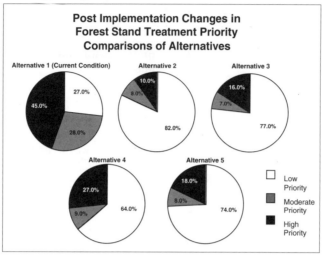

Table II-3: Issue Indicators, Summary Comparison of Alternatives

Issues	Alternative 1 No Action	Alternative 2 Proposed Action	Alternative 3	Alternative 4	Alternative 5
Issue #1: Sediment Effects to 303(d) streams, Grimes Creek and Mores Creek					
- Sediment Delivery/(MK Model) *(cubic meters/year)-single year highest delivery/compared to sediment delivery, 6 years post project)*					
-Gregory/Johnny 6th Field HUC	25.64	33.78, 1 year peak/return to 18.75	34.05, 1 year peak/return to 18.90	34.05, 1 year peak/return to 18.90	34.05, 1 year peak/return to 18.90
-Lower Elk 6th Field HUC	35.10	63.14, 1 year peak/return to 34.93	63.14, 1 year peak/return to 34.93	63.14, 1 year peak/return to 34.93	63.14, 1 year peak/return to 34.93
-Minneha/Wildcat 6th Field HUC	20.03	24.03, 1 year peak/return to 13.36	24.11, 1 year peak/return to 13.41	24.11, 1 year peak/return to 13.41	24.11, 1 year peak/return to 13.41
-Pine 6th Field HUC	7.33	13.17, 1 year peak/return to 7.32	13.20, 1 year peak/return to 7.33	No peak return to 7.33	13.20, 1 year peak/return to 7.33
-Wild Goat/Deadhorse 6th Field HUC	12.52	18.62, 1 year peak/return to 10.35	18.62, 1 year peak/return to 10.35	No peak return to 12.52	18.62, 1 year peak/return to 10.35
BOISED Model Results *(% over natural, single year-highest peak/compared to post project, year 2007)*					
-Gregory/Johnny 6th Field HUC	15%	46% peak/ return to 12%	44% peak/ return to 11%	21% peak/ return to 12%	21% peak/ return to 12%
-Lower Elk 6th Field HUC	6%	36% peak/ return to 10%	24% peak/ return to 9%	22% peak/ return to 9%	24% peak/ return to 10%
-Minneha/Wildcat 6th Field HUC	21%	65% peak/ return to 21%	56% peak/ return to 21%	26% peak/ return to 21%	46% peak/ return to 21%
-Pine 6th Field HUC	2%	44% peak/ return to 4%	42% peak/ return to 3%	3% peak/ return to 2%	3% peak/ return to 2%
-Wild Goat/Deadhorse 6th Field HUC	9%	27% peak/ return to 13%	23% peak/ return to 12%	11% peak/ return to 11%	21% peak/ return to 12%

EXAMPLE **2.4.1–1** (continued).

Table II-4: Other Resource Indicators, Summary Comparison of Alternatives

Other Resource Indicators	Alternative 1 No Action	Alternative 2 Proposed Action	Alternative 3	Alternative 4	Alternative 5
Fisheries					
-INFISH Habitat RMOs	Compliant	Compliant	Compliant	Compliant	Compliant
-TES Fish Species	No Effect	No Effect	No Effect	No Effect	No Effect
Wildlife					
TES Wildlife Species (3)	No Effect	1. "May affect, not likely to adversely affect" (*Gray Wolf*) 2. "May affect, not likely to jeopardize the continued existence of the species" (*Canada Lynx*)			
Sensitive Species (12)	No Impacts	Beneficial Impact (2 species)			
MIS (3)	No Effect	Beneficial Impact (elk)	Beneficial Impact (elk)	No Effect	No Effect
Rare Plants - T&E Plants (1) - Sensitive Plants (5) - Forest Concern Plants (6)	No Effect to any rare plant species	MIIH* for 2 species (1 Sensitive, 1 Forest Concern)			
Cultural Resources	No Effect	# - see note below			
Recreation Opportunities/Visuals	No change in the short term to vegetative conditions. Increased chance of substantial change to vegetative conditions in the long term.	Minor impacts on recreation use during project activities. Increased chance of sustaining vegetative conditions in the long term			

*MIIH - May Impact Individuals or Habitat, but will n⌐ contribute to a trend towards Federal listing, or loss of viability to the species.

- A "may be adversely affected" determination is no⌐ 1. 4: Cultural Resources. A Memorandum of Agreement (MOA) will be submitted to the State Historic Preservation Officer (SHPO) to esta⌐ ⌐lementation procedures to protect any cultural sites within any management activities area of impact. It is expected that the MOA w⌐ ⌐roved, the potential adverse effects resolved, and that no adverse effects will occur on any cultural resource sites.

EXAMPLE 2.4.1–1 (continued).

TABLE 2.1.–3
COMPARISON OF AIR EMISSION
VALLEY AIR FORCE BASE

AIR POLLUTANTS
(TONS PER YEAR)

Source	Aircraft Sorties Annually	CO	HC	NO$_X$	PM	So$_X$
Baseline	58,866	640	130	320	5.0	65
Proposed Action	389	.1	.4	2	.06	0.4
Baseline and Proposed Action	59,255	640.1	130.4	322	5.06	65.4
Grant County	N/A	5,300	2,014	3,319	459	6,642
Jasper County	N/A	441	463	151	231	20
				%		
Proposed Action as a Percent of Grant County Emissions		.002	.02	.1	.01	.006
Proposed Action as a Percent of Jasper County Emissions		.02	.1	1	.03	2

CO - Carbon Monoxide
HC - Hydrocarbons
NO$_X$ - Oxides of Nitrogen
PM - Particulate Matter
SO$_X$ - Oxides of Sulfur
N/A - Not Applicable

EXAMPLE **2.4.1–2**—*This table, adapted from an EA prepared by the U.S. Air Force, shows the comparative effects of the proposed action vs. the baseline (no action). This information would be only one part of the usual comparative matrix presented in Chapter 2; similar data on other resources would be presented.*

2.4.2 Make the information in the comparative matrix as quantifiable as possible. Record acres disturbed, the number of grazing animals, variations in flow rates, etc. Use such trend words as *high, low, moderate,* and *limited* only if you have carefully explained in Chapter 4 what each of these trend words means. Note that these trend words avoid judgment words like *good, bad,* or *desirable.*

Use phrases, even sentences, in the matrix if you have to qualify or explain either your numerical estimates or your trend words. You must support your judgments (forecasts) with a careful analysis in Chapter 4. Thus, this matrix in Chapter 2 becomes the summary matrix for all of Chapter 4.

2.4.3 Do not use numerical ratings, checkmarks, or other evaluation methods to summarize the effects of the alternatives. See negative example 2.4.3. These methods have the illusion of certainty, but they are less reliable than words like *high* and *low.* If the matrix is properly done, readers cannot mindlessly add up a column or row to find out which alternative is supposedly the best one. Both the decisionmaker and members of the public have to impose their own value systems (trade-offs) on the information in the matrix.

2.5 Identify your agency's preferred alternative, unless your agency directs otherwise. Do not give in the EIS/EA the rationale for your choice. Include the rationale in the ROD or Decision Document/FONSI.

2.5.1 For a Draft EIS, identify your agency's preferred alternative, unless another law prohibits such an identification. The purpose is to tell readers of the Draft EIS what the agency is currently planning to do. This identification allows readers to comment substantively on the agency's likely choice. The agency must respond to these comments when it issues its Final EIS.

2.5.2 For an EA, some agencies do **not** identify a preferred alternative. Other agencies require such an identification and a few even require the rationale.

Usually, the final (finished) EA has a FONSI (Finding of No Significant Impact) and an EA decision document attached to it.

In cases where an agency wants to issue a preliminary or review EA (usually not called a draft EA in order to prevent legal confusion with a draft EIS), consider attaching a cover letter identifying which alternative the decisionmaker intends to select and telling the reader of the EA how to comment or to respond to the EA. Remind readers that this preliminary EA will not be processed like a Draft EIS.

The FONSI will identify the agency's chosen (selected) alternative, so the preferred agency alternative has no role in a final (finished) EA.

2.5.3 Do not include rationale for the chosen, selected, or preferred alternative. The rationale belongs, instead, in the Record of Decision or FONSI (plus EA decision document). See the discussion of the FONSI on pp. 70–74.

If the EIS/EA is carefully written, the decisionmaker can choose any one of the alternatives without requiring a change in the document. For an EIS, only the single sentence identifying the

preferred alternative would change. For an EA, nothing would change; only the FONSI and decision document would change.

Without a rationale (justification), the EIS/EA becomes a technical document that discloses the potential consequences of the alternatives.

Evaluation Techniques to Avoid in a Matrix

		Alternatives			
		A	B	C	D
I S S U E S	Air Quality	-	Good	4	◑
	Water Quality	- -	Great	2	●◑
	Fish Habitat	- - -	Bad	1	◔
	Vegetation	-	Better	3	◕
	Economics	+ +	Good	6	◐
	Social	+	Worst	5	◕

EXAMPLE 2.4.3—*None of the above evaluation techniques should appear in your EIS or EA. Use either quantifications (as in example 2.4.1–2) or other indicators (as in example 2.4.1–1). Using numerical rankings or a plus or minus does not really disclose effects unless you supply a careful rationale for the numerical rating or a plus or minus.*

NOTE: You can use these evaluation techniques as a tool during interdisciplinary team discussions, but these techniques should not be retained in the EA or EIS. Instead, focus the EA or EIS on the written rationale supporting the team's evaluations.

AFFECTED ENVIRONMENT (CHAPTER 3.0)

SUGGESTED CONTENT

3.0 Affected Environment

3.1 Explain that this chapter presents relevant resource components of the existing environment—that is, the baseline environment. As appropriate, preview the chapter contents so that readers can readily find subsections.

3.2 Resource X (Issue 1)

3.3 Resource Y

3.4 Resource Z (Issue 2)

. . .

See Appendix A for examples of how to organize Chapters 3 and 4.

SUGGESTIONS FOR WRITING

3.0 Affected Environment

3.1 Explain that this chapter presents relevant resource components of the existing environment—that is, the baseline environment. As appropriate, preview the chapter contents so that readers can readily find subsections.

3.1.1 Recently, a few agencies have begun combining Chapters 3 and 4. This organizational option allows for all current and future conditions pertinent to a single resource to be discussed in a single subsection.

3.1.2 Chapter 3 is not required for an EA, but if you omit it, you must include the necessary baseline information into your discussions in Chapter 4, Environmental Consequences, which then becomes Chapter 3 of your EA.

3.1.3 Explain that Chapter 3 describes the environmental components (resources) of the area that **would be affected** by the alternatives and that **would affect** the alternatives if they were implemented.

Remind readers that, despite the word *affected* in the title, this chapter does not present effects. Instead, the environment described is the baseline for the comparisons in Chapter 4, Environmental Consequences.

3.1.4 Discuss in detail resources you earlier (in Chapter 1) listed as relevant issues. Your discussion of these issues (resources) should validate why these are deemed to be relevant to the decision to be made.

3.1.5 Discuss as briefly as possible those resources not identified as relevant. In some cases, you might merely list certain resources as considered but not found in the project area. Remember that some things—such as wetlands, threatened and endangered species, or cultural resources—should always be mentioned, if only to note that none exists in the project area.

Such a paragraph listing items considered but not present in the project area provides legal evidence that you have not overlooked any resources.

No matter how you decide in your EIS/EA to cover resources you don't consider relevant, remember to provide backup information as appropriate. Such information could be memos from specialists or a checklist like example 3.1.5. If you decide to use a checklist, include it in the appendix or in the analysis file and be sure to reference it in the EIS/EA.

3.1.6 Sometimes you need to describe parts of the environment that would not be affected by the proposed action or by any alternative. For example, if an earthquake fault was located near the project site, the decisionmaker and the public ought to know of its presence even though the project would not affect the fault. But the fault might affect the project.

3.1.7 Describe the area where the proposed action would take place. Include the legal description if necessary. Probably a general location map appears in Chapter 1; refer to it and include a more specific, detailed map here if needed.

CEQ REGULATIONS

§ 1502.15 Affected environment.

The environmental impact statement shall succinctly describe the environment of the area(s) to be affected or created by the alternatives under consideration. The descriptions shall be no longer than is necessary to understand the effects of the alternatives. Data and analyses in a statement shall be commensurate with the importance of the impact, with less important material summarized, consolidated, or simply referenced. Agencies shall avoid useless bulk in statements and shall concentrate effort and attention on important issues. Verbose descriptions of the affected environment are themselves no measure of the adequacy of an environmental impact statement.

3.1.8 Preview the rest of the chapter by explaining how you have organized the resources. Remind readers that Chapter 3 covers resources in the same order as they will be covered in Chapter 4.

A common organization has been to use general categories: physical, biological, social, and economic. Individual resources become third-level subheadings under the four categories. If you choose to follow this pattern, tell your readers.

Another organization (one we prefer) is to arrange individual resources (issues) according to their relationship to each other or their significance. For instance, hydrology and fisheries would appear next to each other. Such an organization is particularly common if you have only three or four relevant issues; after you cover these three or four, you can move on to brief discussions of the remaining resources.

Environmental Factors Checklist

Directions: Check the appropriate columns to indicate that the interdisciplinary team has addressed each of these factors. For those factors with background documentation, indicate where readers can find the information—in the EA, in the appendices, or in the analysis file. As appropriate, include this checklist in an appendix or in the analysis file.

Factors	In EA	Analyzed, Not in EA	Not Applicable	Background Documentation (Location)
Physical Factors.				
1. Location.	❏	❏	❏	_____
2. Geomorphic/physiographic.	❏	❏	❏	_____
a. Geologic hazards.	❏	❏	❏	_____
b. Unique land forms.	❏	❏	❏	_____
3. Climate.	❏	❏	❏	_____
4. Soils.	❏	❏	❏	_____
a. Productivity.	❏	❏	❏	_____
b. Capability.	❏	❏	❏	_____
(1) Erodibility.	❏	❏	❏	_____
(2) Mass failure.	❏	❏	❏	_____
5. Minerals and energy resources.	❏	❏	❏	_____
a. Locatable minerals.	❏	❏	❏	_____
b. Leasable minerals.	❏	❏	❏	_____
c. Energy sources.	❏	❏	❏	_____
6. Visual resources.	❏	❏	❏	_____
7. Cultural resources.	❏	❏	❏	_____
a. Archaeological.	❏	❏	❏	_____
b. Historical.	❏	❏	❏	_____
c. Architectural.	❏	❏	❏	_____
8. Wilderness resources.	❏	❏	❏	_____
9. Wild and scenic rivers.	❏	❏	❏	_____
10. Water resources.	❏	❏	❏	_____
a. Water quality.	❏	❏	❏	_____
b. Streamflow regimes.	❏	❏	❏	_____
c. Floodplains.	❏	❏	❏	_____
d. Wetlands.	❏	❏	❏	_____
e. Ground water recharge areas.	❏	❏	❏	_____

EXAMPLE 3.1.5—*A checklist is a good tool to validate that you have addressed all potential resources. Always have such a checklist in your analysis file. As an option, put the checklist in the appendix. The above checklist is based on a Forest Service list of environmental factors.*

Factors	In EA	Analyzed, Not in EA	Not Applicable	Background Documentation (Location)
11. Air quality.	❑	❑	❑	_____
12. Noise.	❑	❑	❑	_____
13. Fire.	❑	❑	❑	_____
a. Potential wildfire hazard.	❑	❑	❑	_____
b. Role of fire in the ecosystem.	❑	❑	❑	_____
14. Land use including prime farm, timber, and rangelands.	❑	❑	❑	_____
15. Infrastructure improvements.	❑	❑	❑	_____
a. Roads.	❑	❑	❑	_____
b. Trails.	❑	❑	❑	_____
c. Utility corridors and distribution.	❑	❑	❑	_____
d. Water collection, storage.	❑	❑	❑	_____
e. Communications systems.	❑	❑	❑	_____
f. Solid waste collection and disposal.	❑	❑	❑	_____
Biological Factors.				
1. Vegetation.	❑	❑	❑	_____
a. Forest, including diversity of tree species.	❑	❑	❑	_____
b. Rangeland, including conditions and trends.	❑	❑	❑	_____
c. Other major vegetation types.	❑	❑	❑	_____
d. Threatened or endangered plants.	❑	❑	❑	_____
e. Research natural area (RNA) potentials.	❑	❑	❑	_____
f. Unique ecosystems (other than RNAs).	❑	❑	❑	_____
g. Diversity of plant communities.	❑	❑	❑	_____
h. Noxious weeds.	❑	❑	❑	_____

EXAMPLE 3.1.5 (continued).

Factors	In EA	Analyzed, Not in EA	Not Applicable	Background Documentation (Location)
2. Wildlife.	❏	❏	❏	_____
a. Habitat.	❏	❏	❏	_____
b. Populations.	❏	❏	❏	_____
c. Threatened or endangered species.	❏	❏	❏	_____
d. Diversity of animal communities.	❏	❏	❏	_____
e. Animal damage control.	❏	❏	❏	_____
3. Fish.	❏	❏	❏	_____
a. Habitat.	❏	❏	❏	_____
b. Populations.	❏	❏	❏	_____
c. Threatened or endangered species, including State-listed species.	❏	❏	❏	_____
4. Recreation resources (usually a combination of physical and biological factors).	❏	❏	❏	_____
5. Insects and diseases.	❏	❏	❏	_____
6. Exotic organisms; for example, Russian thistle, Siberian ibex.	❏	❏	❏	_____
Economic Factors.				
1. Economic base.	❏	❏	❏	_____
2. Employment/unemployment.	❏	❏	❏	_____
3. Housing.	❏	❏	❏	_____
4. Land use requirements.	❏	❏	❏	_____
5. Community service requirements.	❏	❏	❏	_____
6. Revenue base.	❏	❏	❏	_____
a. Local general government.	❏	❏	❏	_____
b. Special service districts.	❏	❏	❏	_____
7. Plans and programs of other agencies.	❏	❏	❏	_____
8. Income.	❏	❏	❏	_____
a. Sources.	❏	❏	❏	_____
b. Amounts.	❏	❏	❏	_____
c. Distribution.	❏	❏	❏	_____
9. Cost.	❏	❏	❏	_____
a. Financial analysis (who pays for what, when).	❏	❏	❏	_____

EXAMPLE 3.1.5 (continued).

Factors	In EA	Analyzed, Not in EA	Not Applicable	Background Documentation (Location)
Social Factors.				
1. Population dynamics.	❏	❏	❏	_____
a. Size (growth, stability, decline).	❏	❏	❏	_____
b. Composition (age, sex, minority).	❏	❏	❏	_____
c. Distribution and density.	❏	❏	❏	_____
d. Mobility.	❏	❏	❏	_____
e. Displacement.	❏	❏	❏	_____
2. Social institutions.	❏	❏	❏	_____
a. Educational.	❏	❏	❏	_____
b. Family.	❏	❏	❏	_____
c. Economic.	❏	❏	❏	_____
d. Political.	❏	❏	❏	_____
e. Military.	❏	❏	❏	_____
f. Religious.	❏	❏	❏	_____
g. Recreation/leisure.	❏	❏	❏	_____
3. Special concerns.	❏	❏	❏	_____
a. Minority (civil rights).	❏	❏	❏	_____
b. Environmental justice.	❏	❏	❏	_____
c. Historic/archaeological/ cultural.	❏	❏	❏	_____
4. Ways of life—defined by.	❏	❏	❏	_____
a. Subcultural variation.	❏	❏	❏	_____
b. Leisure and cultural opportunities.	❏	❏	❏	_____
c. Subsistence hunting and fishing.	❏	❏	❏	_____
d. Personal security.	❏	❏	❏	_____
e. Stability and change.	❏	❏	❏	_____
f. Basic values.	❏	❏	❏	_____
g. Symbolic meaning.	❏	❏	❏	_____
h. Cohesion and conflict.	❏	❏	❏	_____
i. Community identity.	❏	❏	❏	_____
j. Health and safety.	❏	❏	❏	_____
5. Land tenure and land use.	❏	❏	❏	_____
6. Legal considerations.	❏	❏	❏	_____

EXAMPLE 3.1.5 (continued).

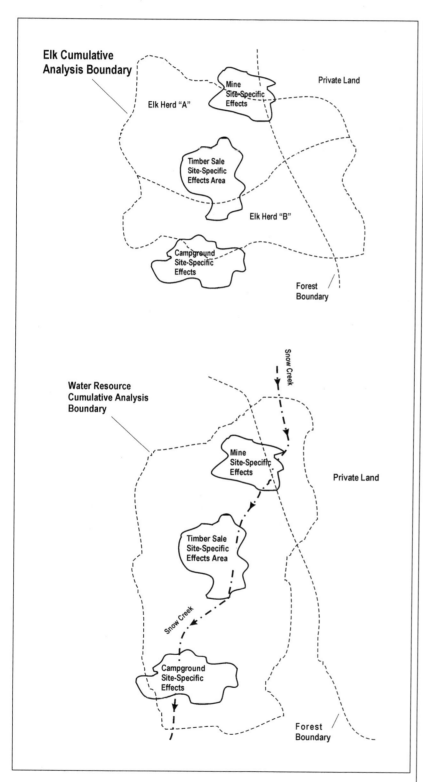

3.2 Resource X (Issue 1)

3.2.1 Cross-reference each resource with its parallel issue (from Chapter 1). At times, your discussion of a resource may include more implications than you chose to introduce in Chapter 1. Even so, cross-reference between the chapters. Your goal is to help your readers see the links between relevant issues and resources.

Particularly important are the indicators you mentioned for each issue discussed in Chapter 1. If, for example, you identified ram/ewe ratios as important to the viability of the bighorn sheep population, record in this chapter the current ram/ewe ratios in the project area.

3.2.2 Describe what **is,** not what **would be.** Don't include effects; effects appear in Chapter 4 (Environmental Consequences). Although your emphasis is on what is, you also should mention any trend that is apparent from available data. For example, surveys may have shown that the grazing on a particular allotment has declined in recent years. Record this trend as part of the current baseline information.

3.2.3 Stipulate the area you are describing for each affected resource because the area of potential cumulative effects will differ from resource to resource. Thus, your baseline area for one resource will often extend beyond the project area you described at the beginning of this chapter and in Chapter 1. You cannot determine the proper resource area to describe until you finish analyzing the potential cumulative effects of all alternatives.

The maps in example 3.2.3 illustrate how different cumulative analysis

EXAMPLE 3.2.3—*Each resource you analyze should have its own map showing the extent of the analysis.*

boundaries apply to different resources. You should include such adjusted or extended area maps for each resource. Also, explain why (and how) the area differs from the project area described in Chapter 1.

See *FCSG—Maps*

3.2.4 Incorporate by reference relevant information. As in example 3.2.4, briefly summarize all information that you incorporate by reference. Information you incorporate by reference must be reasonably available to the public.

Use parenthetical citations rather than footnotes to cite references.

See *FCSG—Citations*

See *FCSG—Bibliographies*

All references cited should appear in an alphabetical list in the bibliography. See the discussion of the bibliography on p. 67.

Parenthetical references should include the page number, preceded by the abbreviations *p.* for *page* and *pp.* for *pages*. Some Federal agencies and some scientific disciplines are beginning to use the single abbreviation *p.* for both *page* and *pages*. If you choose to use the single form of the abbreviation, do so throughout your entire EIS or EA.

CEQ REGULATIONS

§ 1502.21 Incorporation by reference.

Agencies shall incorporate material into an environmental impact statement by reference when the effect will be to cut down on bulk without impeding agency and public review of the action. The incorporated material shall be cited in the statement and its content briefly described. No material may be incorporated by reference unless it is reasonably available for inspection by potentially interested persons within the time allowed for comment. Material based on proprietary data which is itself not available for review and comment shall not be incorporated by reference.

According to recent studies (Jones 1986, pp. 234–237, and Clarkson 1988, pp. 45–46), lamb survival depends directly on the nutritional value of browse available to ewes, which itself is a function of the moisture available from early spring through June.

EXAMPLE 3.2.4—*Use parenthetical citations, not footnotes, to cite referenced information. Also, be sure to summarize briefly the relevant content.*

3.2.5 Use graphics, whenever possible, to capture key concepts and complex relationships. Graphics are usually most effective when they are designed for a specific EIS/EA, not drawn from some tangential research study or report.

⮕ See *FCSG—Graphics for Documents*

Both examples 3.2.5–1 and 3.2.5–2 show how project-specific concepts can be presented in graphics. Remember to plan (design) your graphics early because they may replace sections of the text.

3.3 Resource Y

3.3.1 Cover resources that may not be relevant issues. Resource Y is such a resource. The procedural (legal) requirement is that you develop a clear legal record for all potentially affected resources.

Resource Y, for instance, might be a resource that started out as a relevant issue (in the analysis process). During the analysis, however, the interdisciplinary team managed to adjust the potential alternatives so that effects on Resource Y became minimal for all alternatives. Still, some effects remain. So Resource Y is retained in Chapter 3 (and Chapter 4) even though the discussions are appropriately brief.

3.3.2 Keep the discussion of issues that are not relevant brief by referencing either appendices or the analysis file. Such references should be specific for each resource and should indicate what readers would find if they turned to the appendices or examined the analysis file.

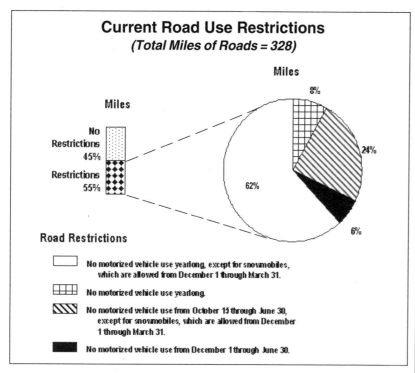

Current Road Use Restrictions
(Total Miles of Roads = 328)

Miles

Miles

No Restrictions 45%

Restrictions 55%

8%

24%

62%

6%

Road Restrictions

☐ No motorized vehicle use yearlong, except for snowmobiles, which are allowed from December 1 through March 31.

▦ No motorized vehicle use yearlong.

▨ No motorized vehicle use from October 15 through June 30, except for snowmobiles, which are allowed from December 1 through March 31.

■ No motorized vehicle use from December 1 through June 30.

EXAMPLE 3.2.5–1—*A graphic such as this one can replace a number of lines of text. As in this example, graphics can have a caption (headline) above them. More commonly, both the title and caption appear under the graphic.*

3.4 Resource Z (Issue 2)

3.4.1 Resource Z, like Resource X, is linked to a relevant issue introduced in Chapter 1. Use such cross-references throughout your EIS/EA.

3.4.2 As with any resource linked to a relevant issue, discuss it in appropriate detail. Avoid, however, overloading the discussion with background (file) information that is better summarized and then referenced. A good rule of thumb is that any information in Chapter 3 should be directly related to the environmental consequences to be presented in Chapter 4.

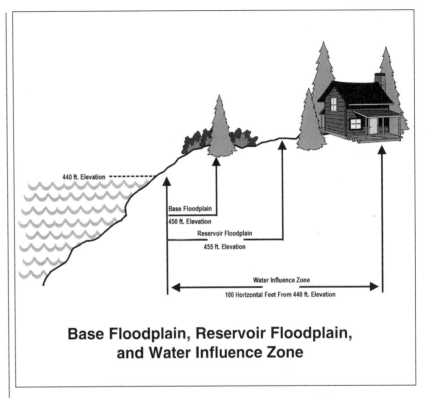

Base Floodplain, Reservoir Floodplain, and Water Influence Zone

EXAMPLE 3.2.5.–2—*This graphic essentially defines three different areas around a proposed reservoir. The accompanying text would, of course, explain the technical assumptions supporting these definitions.*

ENVIRONMENTAL CONSEQUENCES (CHAPTER 4.0)

SUGGESTED CONTENT

Sections with an asterisk (*) are usually retained in an EA; the others arc omitted or combined with other sections.

Remember, your organization should parallel the one you chose for Chapter 3.

*4.0 Environmental Consequences
(organizational option 1)

*4.1 Explain that this chapter is organized by resources.

*4.2 Effects on Resource X
(Issue 1)
4.2.1 Alternative A (No Action)
4.2.2 Alternative B (Proposed Action)
4.2.3 Alternative C (Short Title)
4.2.4 Alternative D (Short Title)

Choose organizational option 1 if you have an EIS or a lengthy EA.

*4.3 Effects on Resource Y
4.3.1 Alternative A (No Action)
4.3.2 Alternative B (Proposed Action)
4.3.3 Alternative C (Short Title)
4.4.4 Alternative D (Short Title)

Choose option 2 if you have a short EA or you want to emphasize alternatives.

*4.4 Effects on Resource Z
(Issue 2)
. . .

*4.10 Unavoidable Adverse Effects
*4.11 Relationship of Short-Term Uses and Long-Term Productivity
*4.12 Irreversible and Irretrievable Commitments of Resources
*4.13 Any Other Disclosures

*4.0 Environmental Consequences
(organizational option 2)

*4.1 Explain that this chapter is arranged by alternatives.

*4.2 Effects of Alternative A
(No Action)
4.2.1 Resource X (Issue 1)
4.2.2 Resource Y
4.2.3 Resource Z (Issue 2)
. . .

*4.3 Effects of Alternative B
(Proposed Action)
4.3.1 Resource X (Issue 1)
4.3.2 Resource Y
4.3.3 Resource Z (Issue 2)
. . .

*4.10 Unavoidable Adverse Effects
*4.11 Relationship of Short-Term Uses and Long-Term Productivity
*4.12 Irreversible and Irretrievable Commitments of Resources
*4.13 Any Other Disclosures

SUGGESTIONS FOR WRITING

*4.0 Environmental Consequences (organizational option 1)

  *4.1 Explain that this chapter is organized by resources.

or

*4.0 Environmental Consequences (organizational option 2)

  *4.1. Explain that this chapter is organized by alternatives.

4.1.1 Introduce this chapter by explaining that it is "the scientific and analytic basis for the comparisons" of the alternatives. Explain that this section describes the probable consequences (impacts, effects) of each alternative on selected environmental resources.

4.1.2 Choose a chapter organization to fit your project and the scope of your EIS/EA.

  If you are writing an EIS (or long EA) and if you have fairly well-developed technical analyses of the probable consequences, organize by resources (organizational option 1). Choosing this organization allows each technical area to develop its own discussion and its own methodologies. This option more closely fits with the "scientific and analytic" intent of this chapter.

If you are writing a short EA and if you have limited technical information, organize by alternatives (organizational option 2). This organization is appropriate if you have brief profiles of the consequences related to each alternative. The more technical information you have on each resource, the more desirable is option 1— organizing by resource.

4.1.3 Tell your readers which organizational option you have chosen. Remind them that Chapter 4 will discuss resources in the same sequence as they were discussed in Chapter 3.

See Appendix A for examples of how to organize Chapters 3 and 4.

CEQ REGULATIONS

§ 1502.16 Environmental consequences.

This section forms the scientific and analytic basis for the comparisons under § 1502.14. It shall consolidate the discussions of those elements required by sections 102(2)(C) (i), (ii), (iv), and (v) of NEPA which are within the scope of the statement and as much of section 102(2)(C)(iii) as is necessary to support the comparisons. The discussion will include the environmental impacts of the alternatives including the proposed action, any adverse environmental effects which cannot be avoided should the proposal be implemented, the relationship between short-term uses of man's environment and the maintenance and enhancement of long-term productivity, and any irreversible or irretrievable commitments of resources which would be involved in the proposal should it be implemented. This section should not duplicate discussions in § 1502.14. It shall include discussions of:

(a) Direct effects and their significance (§ 1508.18).
(b) Indirect effects and their significance (§ 1508.8).
(c) Possible conflicts between the proposed action and the objectives of Federal, regional, State, and local (and in the case of a reservation, Indian tribe) land use plans, policies and controls for the area concerned. (See § 1506.2(d).)
(d) The environmental effects of alternatives including the proposed action. The comparisons under § 1502.14 will be based on this discussion.
(e) Energy requirements and conservation potential of various alternatives and mitigation measures.
(f) Natural or depletable resource requirements and conservation potential of various alternatives and mitigation measures.
(g) Urban quality, historic and cultural resources, and the design of the built environment, including the reuse and conservation potential of various alternatives and mitigation measures.
(h) Means to mitigate adverse environmental impacts (if not fully covered under § 1502.14(f)).

No new mitigation in chapt 4 introduced in chap. 2

NOTE: Add cumulative impacts to the list of topics to be discussed under CEQ § 1502.16.

*4.2 Effects on Resource X (Issue 1)

4.2.1 Alternative A (No Action)

or

*4.2 Effects of Alternative A (No Action)

4.2.1 Resource X (Issue 1)

4.2.1 In either organization, you must address the effects of each alternative on **all** relevant resources. The challenge is to cover all potential effects (impacts) that are relevant to the decision: direct, indirect, cumulative, short-term, long-term, beneficial, and adverse. You also need to identify any irreversible and irretrievable commitments. These categories overlap, making any discussion of them difficult to organize.

For conceptual purposes, use the checklist in example 4.2.1 to guarantee that you haven't overlooked the major effects. Note that each item in this checklist could be a subheading, or you might decide to combine items under a single subheading (for example, past, present, and future cumulative effects).

4.2.2 Cover all affected resources, but focus more detailed discussions on resources linked to the relevant issues identified in Chapter 1. Also, as CEQ § 1502.16 indicates, some things like energy requirements, conservation potential, and cultural resources might be mentioned in Chapter 4 even if they aren't relevant issues.

Remember that all mitigations (topic (h) in CEQ § 1502.16) should already be included in one or more action alternatives. All mitigations tracked in an EIS or EA should be introduced in Chapter 2. Then Chapter 4 presents the impacts assuming mitigations occur.

Effects on Resource X

❑ Analytic, concise introduction to Resource X, including indicators, models, technical assumptions, analysis boundary, and analysis intensity

❑ Direct and indirect effects of Alternative B

❑ Total cumulative effects of all actions (including Alternative B)

  ❑ Effects of past connected and cumulative actions

  ❑ Effects of present connected and cumulative actions

  ❑ Effects of reasonably foreseeable future connected and cumulative actions

❑ Other potential effects (if not already covered and discussed)

  ❑ Adverse effects that cannot be avoided

  ❑ Short-term uses vs. long-term productivity

  ❑ Irreversible and irretrievable commitments

EXAMPLE **4.2.1**—*Use this checklist for each resource and each alternative to guarantee that you've considered all potential impacts. The items in the checklist need not be separate subheadings. In many documents, for example, cumulative effects would not be broken out into past, present, and future.*

Be sure to analyze all direct and indirect effects. Do not, however, try to separate direct from indirect effects when you organize the headings in this chapter.

4.2.3 Conceptually, begin with actions (causes) and then analyze the potential effects (both direct and indirect).

The line between direct and indirect is difficult to draw and somewhat arbitrary; the key is to be sure that you have covered all relevant, meaningful direct and indirect effects. The flow chart in example 4.2.3 illustrates how different effects flow from a single action (cause). You should also prioritize the possible effects so that you focus on those that are most important to adequate NEPA disclosure.

The flow chart presents more detail than you would need in your EIS/EA, but use the same conceptual approach to guarantee that you haven't overlooked any possible effects. What you choose to discuss in the EIS/EA will depend on the indicators you decide to display and track for each relevant issue.

CEQ REGULATIONS

§ 1508.8 Effects.

"Effects" include:

(a) Direct effects, which are caused by the action and occur at the same time and place.

(b) Indirect effects, which are caused by the action and are later in time or farther removed in distance, but are still reasonably foreseeable. Indirect effects may include growth inducing effects and other effects related to induced changes in the pattern of land use, population density or growth rate, and related effects on air and water and other natural systems, including ecosystems.

Effects and impacts as used in these regulations are synonymous. Effects include ecological (such as the effects on natural resources and on the components, structures, and functioning of affected ecosystems), aesthetic, historic, cultural, economic, social, or health, whether direct, indirect, or cumulative. Effects may also include those resulting from actions which may have both beneficial and detrimental effects, even if on balance the agency believes that the effect will be beneficial.

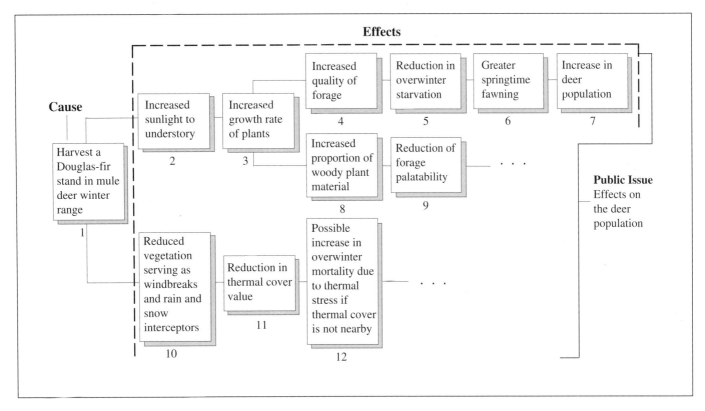

EXAMPLE 4.2.3—*This flow chart schematically captures the cause-and-effect relationship behind the public issue of the effects on the deer population. Note that the initial cause (the harvest of Douglas-fir stand) potentially has both beneficial and adverse effects. In this flow chart, we have not attempted to separate direct from indirect effects. In an EIS or EA you must discuss all effects, but you need not separate them into direct and indirect categories. NOTE: the numbers under each box are for reference purposes; they do not indicate the sequence of the effects.*

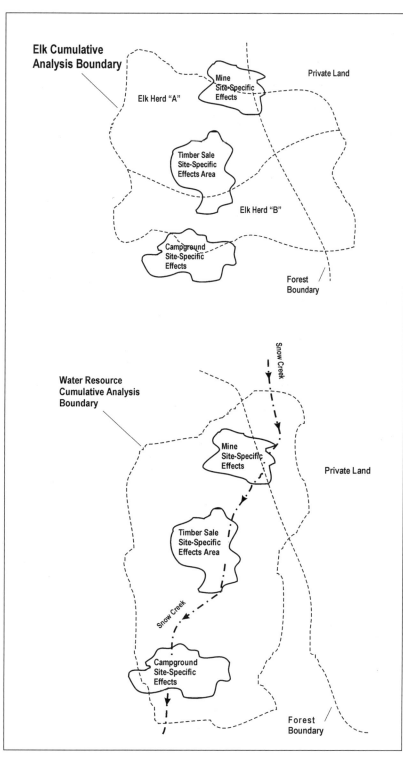

Elk Cumulative
Analysis Boundary

Mine
Site-Specific
Effects

Private Land

Elk Herd "A"

Timber Sale
Site-Specific
Effects Area

Elk Herd "B"

Campground
Site-Specific
Effects

Forest
Boundary

Water Resource
Cumulative Analysis
Boundary

Snow Creek

Mine
Site-Specific
Effects

Private Land

Timber Sale
Site-Specific
Effects Area

Snow Creek

Campground
Site-Specific
Effects

Forest
Boundary

EXAMPLE 4.2.4–1—*Each resource will likely have a different cumulative analysis boundary. Either here in Chapter 4 or earlier in Chapter 3, you should provide maps of the analysis boundary for each resource.*

4.2.4 Stipulate the geographical and temporal boundaries (the context) for your analysis of each resource. These boundaries do not coincide with the project boundaries, which usually reflect only the area and time period when the potential actions would occur.

The maps in example 4.2.4–1 illustrate how different cumulative analysis boundaries apply to different resources. In Chapter 3, you should have included such adjusted or extended area maps for each resource. If appropriate, repeat such maps in Chapter 4, along with any supporting explanations of how the effects discussed in this chapter determine the area to be analyzed.

See *FCSG—Maps*

Temporal boundaries are similarly complex. In example 4.2.4–2, different actions related to a timber sale have different effects, which have different durations.

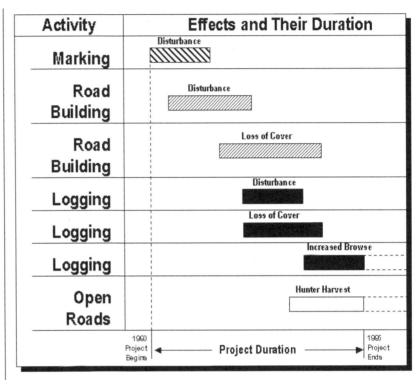

EXAMPLE 4.2.4–2—*Each resource has its own temporal limits. Be sure to specify those for each resource you discuss. The dotted lines for logging and open roads indicate that the effects continue into the future.*

Effects of Alternative 2 on Threatened and Endangered Species

This alternative would proceed with approximately 11,113 acres of timber stand harvest, and construct 61 miles of new roads within the DA (Decision Area).

These activities would reduce the effective habitat within the DA for **grizzly bear** and **wolf** by 29.2 square miles, or 6.3% of the Decision Area (Appendix A). Significant increased human activity and access would occur on this 29.2 square miles of previously available habitat during active sales and road building. Activities would affect all six BMUs (Bear Management Units). Use by grizzlies and wolves of habitat in these activity areas would decrease. This alternative has the second highest amount of human activities and disturbances of those displayed.

Road closures in the DA would more than compensate for increased human activity. Figure 4–78 provides information on the present grizzly bear habitat effectiveness, the effect on habitat effectiveness if road closures were not implemented, and the effect with road closures.

Compensation for the proposed activities would require road closures outside the sale areas to manage grizzly bear habitat at management plan levels (Appendix A). It would also require some winter-season-only sales. Vehicle access and associated human numbers would be reduced on the 29.2 square miles closed to compensate for sale activities. Deliberate or accidental man-caused mortality might decrease in these closed areas.

This alternative would convert 11,113 acres of forested lands (which includes 242 acres of riparian harvesting) to open forage lands, and 230 acres of forested lands to roadways. The total amount of cover to be converted to foraging units within the Decision Area by BMU would be as follows: BMU 11: 866 acres (3%); BMU 13: 681 acres (3%); BMU 14: 2,114 acres (7%); BMU 15: 1,449 acres (3%); BMU 16: 462 acres (7%); and BMU 17: 720 acres (5%). See Appendix A for further details about this conversion of cover to forage.

EXAMPLE **4.2.5**—*Impacts on grizzly bears and wolves are estimated using the percent of effective habitat. These percents (a quantification) are only an indirect measure of the potential impacts. Such indirect indicators are often the only way to estimate effects.*

4.2.5 Quantify effects and interpret your estimated effects. Your discussion should include acres of habitat lost, amount of sediment entering the stream, and other commonly accepted ways to quantify effects on a resource. If you can only indicate effects as trends (*low, moderate, high,* etc.), remember that both quantifications and trends require careful explanation and interpretation.

As in example 4.2.5, you must explain the context and intensity behind your analysis. See CEQ § 1508.27.

4.2.6 Be cautious about using the words *significant* or *significantly.* If you use either of these words, you must explain as precisely as you can, in terms of the context and intensity of the effects, exactly how you are using the term.

In an EIS, your use of *significant* or *significantly* is a proper indication that the agency is disclosing significant impacts (the basic purpose for writing an EIS). Don't, however, label an impact as *significant* without a clear reason for doing so. Unjustified uses of *significant* might establish a legal precedent in future EISs or EAs.

In an EA, however, the use of *significant* or *significantly* about even a single resource will signal in a legal context that the EA should have been an EIS.

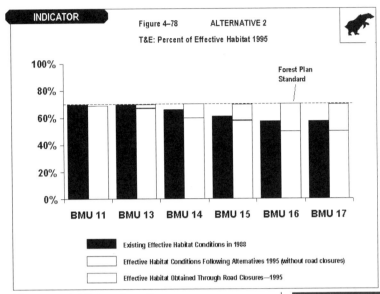

EXAMPLE 4.2.5 (continued).

CEQ REGULATIONS

§ 1508.27 Significantly.

"Significantly" as used in NEPA requires considerations of both context and intensity:

(a) *Context.* This means that the significance of an action must be analyzed in several contexts such as society as a whole (human, national), the affected region, the affected interests, and the locality. Significance varies with the setting of the proposed action. For instance, in the case of a site-specific action, significance would usually depend upon the effects in the locale rather than in the world as a whole. Both short- and long-term effects are relevant.

(b) *Intensity.* This refers to the severity of impact. Responsible officials must bear in mind that more than one agency may make decisions about partial aspects of a major action. The following should be considered in evaluating intensity:

(1) Impacts that may be both beneficial and adverse. A significant effect may exist even if the Federal agency believes that on balance the effect will be beneficial.

(2) The degree to which the proposed action affects public health or safety.

(3) Unique characteristics of the geographic area such as proximity to historic or cultural resources, park lands, prime farmlands, wetlands, wild and scenic rivers, or ecologically critical areas.

(4) The degree to which the effects on the quality of the human environment are likely to be highly controversial.

Continued

CEQ REGULATIONS

§1508.27 Significantly. (continued)

(5) The degree to which the possible effects on the human environment are highly uncertain or involve unique or unknown risks.

(6) The degree to which the action may establish a precedent for future actions with significant effects or represents a decision in principle about a future consideration.

(7) Whether the action is related to other actions with individually insignificant but cumulatively significant impacts. Significance exists if it is reasonable to anticipate a cumulatively significant impact on the environment. Significance cannot be avoided by terming an action temporary or by breaking it down into small component parts.

(8) The degree to which the action may adversely affect districts, sites, highways, structures, or objects listed in or eligible for listing in the National Register of Historic Places or may cause loss or destruction of significant scientific, cultural, or historical resources.

(9) The degree to which the action may adversely affect an endangered or threatened species or its habitat that has been determined to be critical under the Endangered Species Act of 1973.

(10) Whether the action threatens a violation of Federal, State, or local law or requirements imposed for the protection of the environment.

CEQ REGULATIONS

§ 1508.7 Cumulative impact.

"Cumulative impact" is the impact on the environment which results from the incremental impact of the action when added to other past, present, and reasonably foreseeable future actions regardless of what agency (Federal or non-Federal) or person undertakes such other actions. Cumulative impacts can result from individually minor but collectively significant actions taking place over a period of time.

4.2.7 Discuss the cumulative effects of each alternative. (Review CEQ § 1508.7.) Given the legal importance of cumulative effects to an adequate NEPA analysis, consider using a subheading of "Cumulative Effects" for each resource and each alternative. Use this subheading even when all you have to say is that you have identified no cumulative effects.

4.2.8 Defining cumulative effects is an evolving and complex skill. No one knows how far back in the history of a project area to go in determining why the area looks as it does today. And no one can guarantee that all "reasonably foreseeable future actions" have been addressed. Still, NEPA mandates that agencies look at all potential impacts, including those considered cumulative, as defined in CEQ § 1508.7.

Two options exist for presenting cumulative effects in an EIS or EA: (1) define the current baseline conditions as broadly as necessary to include the cumulative perspective or (2) develop a new alternative that presents a second baseline (usually what the project area looked like in its pristine or untouched state).

The first option (one we recommend) is that resource specialists define the current baseline conditions as broadly as necessary. Specialists need initially to determine, if possible, how the project area looked prior to developments or what future changes are reasonably foreseeable. Next, specialists need to stipulate how much and what kind of cumulative information is relevant to the agency's potential decision. Such a stipulation necessarily depends on what are the reasonable alternatives open to the agency's decisionmaker.

Two examples illustrate how this first option would work. In the first example, an agency proposes a project that would affect a wetland that has been degraded but still has value as a wetland. The agency decisionmaker should know how the original wetland looked before approving any further changes to this wetland. The decisionmaker should also know if nearby landowners are proposing actions that might further degrade the wetland. So cumulative information is important.

In a second example, cumulative historical information may be outside the bounds of reasonableness. Consider a case where prior developments in a project area have destroyed an entire wetland. No wetland values now exist, and reclaiming any wetland values is unlikely given the pattern of land ownership and the degree of development. Cumulative historical information about the now-vanished wetlands does not contribute to a reasonable alternative, and the agency should so stipulate in its EIS or EA. In this case, wetlands would not even be a major issue.

The second option (one we do <u>not</u> recommend) is to develop a new baseline alternative (the pristine condition) to replace the traditional no action alternative (usually defined as the current management situation). Two problems arise if an agency tries to use the pristine conditions as the baseline. First, historical records about the pristine conditions may be either inaccurate or missing. Secondly, language in NEPA implies and agencies assume that project activities are properly within their legal authority. So actions designed to return to the pristine pre-development conditions are not a reasonable alternative and are, therefore, outside the usual scope of a NEPA analysis.

4.2.9 Analyze the effects of **all** reasonable alternatives, as identified in Chapter 2. Under no action, both nature and humans cause things to happen, so do not rely on "no effects" (or zeros) as your analysis for the no action alternative.

4.2.10 Assess the effectiveness of all mitigations and management requirements built into each alternative. This assessment is crucial because without it, the actual effects of the various alternatives will not be clear to readers. Therefore, the meaningful effects of an alternative are those that remain after all the actions and mitigations have been taken.

No action has environmental consequences (usually both beneficial and adverse).

The assessment of effectiveness is a technical analysis—not a discussion of budgetary problems. Your assumption is that all mitigations listed in the alternatives (Chapter 2) will occur.

CEQ REGULATIONS

§ 1508.20 Mitigation.

"Mitigation" includes:
   (a) Avoiding the impact altogether by not taking a certain action or parts of an action.
   (b) Minimizing impacts by limiting the degree or magnitude of the action and its implementation.
   (c) Rectifying the impact by repairing, rehabilitating, or restoring the affected environment.
   (d) Reducing or eliminating the impact over time by preservation and maintenance operations during the life of the action.
   (e) Compensating for the impact by replacing or providing substitute resources or environments.

CEQ REGULATIONS

§ 1502.22 Incomplete or unavailable information.

When an agency is evaluating reasonably foreseeable significant adverse effects on the human environment in an environmental impact statement and there is incomplete or unavailable information, the agency shall always make clear that such information is lacking.

(a) If the incomplete information relevant to reasonably foreseeable significant adverse impacts is essential to a reasoned choice among alternatives and the overall costs of obtaining it are not exorbitant, the agency shall include the information in the environmental impact statement.

(b) If the information relevant to reasonably foreseeable significant adverse impacts cannot be obtained because the overall costs of obtaining it are exorbitant or the means to obtain it are not known, the agency shall include within the environmental impact statement: (1) a statement that such information is incomplete or unavailable; (2) a statement of the relevance of the incomplete or unavailable information to evaluating reasonably foreseeable significant adverse impacts on the human environment; (3) a summary of existing credible scientific evidence which is relevant to evaluating the reasonably foreseeable significant adverse impacts on the human environment; and (4) the agency's evaluation of such impacts based upon theoretical approaches or research methods generally accepted in the scientific community. For the purposes of this section, "reasonably foreseeable" includes impacts which have catastrophic consequences, even if their probability of occurrence is low, provided that the analysis of the impacts is supported by credible scientific evidence, is not based on pure conjecture, and is within the rule of reason.

(c) The amended regulation will be applicable to all environmental impact statements for which a Notice of Intent (40 CFR 1508.22) is published in the FEDERAL REGISTER on or after May 27, 1986. For environmental impact statements in progress, agencies may choose to comply with the requirements of either the original or amended regulation.

Alternative A **would** cost about $400,000 the first year because the man-made improvements **would** be removed.

Alternative B **would** cost about $100,000 the first year. The man-made improvements **would** remain and **would** be modified to blend with the landscape.

EXAMPLE **4.2.12**—*Use* would, *not* will, *to forecast actions and effects under all alternatives.*

4.2.11 Identify and explain instances where you have incomplete or unavailable data or where your confidence level is extremely low. Your task is to give an honest and realistic appraisal of the effects on all resources, even when you cannot quantify, when you do not have good data, and when your confidence is low.

4.2.12 As in example 4.2.12, describe what *would be*, not what *will be*. This use of *would* for all alternatives implies that the agency has not already chosen one of the alternatives. (Shift to *will* when you write either the Record of Decision or the Finding of No Significant Impact.)

Would is only one of several verbs that suggest future probability: *would*, *could*, and *might*. *Would* implies a high degree of certainty and is your best choice for making firm forecasts in Chapter 4 of an EIS or EA.

Use *should*, a word historically related to preceding words, only to state an "ethical or moral obligation." Do not use *should* to convey future probabilities.

 See FCSG—Word Problems

According to recent studies (Jones 1986, pp. 234–237, and Clarkson 1988, pp. 45–46), lamb survival depends directly on the nutritional value of browse available to ewes, which itself is a function of the moisture available from early spring through June.

EXAMPLE **4.2.13**—*Careful citations to sources make your discussions more credible.*

4.2.13 Incorporate by reference any relevant information. Chapters 3 and 4 are the primary chapters where you would need to incorporate references to technical information. Briefly summarize all information that you incorporate by reference. Information you incorporate by reference must be reasonably available to the public. (CEQ § 1502.21 is reprinted on p. 43.)

Use parenthetical citations rather than footnotes to cite references, as illustrated in example 4.2.13.

Parenthetical references should include the page number, preceded by the abbreviations *p.* for *page* and *pp.* for *pages*. Some Federal agencies and some scientific disciplines are beginning to use the single abbreviation *p.* for both *page* and *pages*. If you choose to use the single form of the abbreviation, do so throughout your entire EIS or EA.

*4.3 Effects on Resource Y

4.3.1 Alternative A (No Action)

4.3.2 Alternative B (Proposed Action)

4.3.3 Alternative C (Short Title)

4.3.4 Alternative D (Short Title)
. . .
or

*4.3 Effects of Alternative B (Proposed Action)

4.3.1 Resource X (Issue 1)

4.3.2 Resource Y

4.3.3 Resource Z (Issue 2)
. . .

*4.4 Effects on Resource Z (Issue 2)
. . .

or

*4.4 Effects of Alternative C (Short Title)
. . .

Sections 4.3, 4.4, and other second-level subheadings continue the organization introduced at the beginning of Chapter 4. In sections 4.3, 4.4, and other subheadings, follow the suggestions for writing presented for section 4.2 (pp. 48–60).

NOTE: The following subsections (4.10, 4.11, 4.12, and 4.13) usually conclude Chapter 4. Their numbering, of course, would change according to the number of resources and alternatives covered earlier in Chapter 4.

As an option, some writers combine the contents of sections 4.10, 4.11, 4.12, and 4.13 into a single section that summarizes these key legal disclosures.

*4.10 Unavoidable Adverse Effects

Under NEPA, an agency does not have to avoid adverse (or even significant) effects. The key is that an agency identify such effects and then disclose them. Hiding them (that is, being silent about them) is a deadly omission in any EIS or EA.

*4.11 Relationship of Short-Term Uses and Long-Term Productivity

The balance (trade-offs) between short-term uses and long-term productivity is the key to this discussion. The decisionmaker and members of the public need to have a clear sense of what

All references cited should appear in an alphabetical list in the bibliography. See the discussion of the bibliography on p. 67.

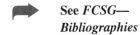 See *FCSG— Bibliographies*

they are gaining or losing in the short term and long term.

The terms *short-term* and *long-term* need definitions consistent with the scope of the proposed project and with resource-specific information. For instance, *long-term* means something quite different in eastern and western U.S. forests. Eastern forests can grow to maturity in 80 to 100 years while many western forests would take two or three times as long. Each resource, of necessity, has to provide its own definitions of *short-term* and *long-term*.

Sections 4.10, 4.11, and 4.12 constitute a key summary of major NEPA disclosure categories.

*4.12   Irreversible and Irretrievable Commitments of Resources

Irreversible and *irretrievable* are confusing because they are not part of everyday language.

Irreversible commitments are those that cannot be reversed, except perhaps in the extreme long term. The classic instance is when a species becomes extinct; this is an irreversible loss. Mining is a similar case; once ore is removed, it can never be replaced. Recent reports suggest that to replace the ecosystem of an old-growth western forest might take 300, 400, or even 500 years. Given the long-term nature of the effects, clear cutting an old-growth forest becomes an irreversible commitment of resources.

Irretrievable commitments are those that are lost for a period of time. If an interstate is constructed through a forest, the timber productivity of the right-of-way is lost for as long as the highway remains. The construction of the highway signals an irretrievable loss in exchange for the benefits of the highway. The highway might also be an irreversible commitment. If a grazing allotment is in poor condition and is likely to remain so, the gap between its current condition and its ideal (potential) productivity is an ongoing irretrievable loss.

*4.13   Any Other Disclosures

Other disclosures vary from agency to agency or department to department.

As CEQ § 1502.16 asks, agencies must disclose energy requirements and conservation measures. If not already covered, agencies should also discuss urban quality and historic and cultural resources. Some agencies also discuss the effects of the proposed action on minorities, consumers, or other potentially affected constituents.

Check your agency procedures for requirements as to these other disclosures.

LIST OF PREPARERS (CHAPTER 5.0)

SUGGESTIONS FOR WRITING

5.0 List of Preparers

5.1 Identify the EIS/EA section(s) written by each individual on the interdisciplinary team. Your analysis file should also contain documentation to show how much the various individuals contributed to the EIS/EA process and to the document.

5.2 As appropriate, distinguish between core team members and specialists who contributed only backup studies or data. Also, indicate team members and specialists who are no longer assigned to the project or employed by the agency.

5.3 Supply brief resumes, highlighting the expertise or experience that lends the most credibility to the sections written by each person. Usually, you should give each person's academic degrees and years of experience with the agency.

5.4 Identify specialists or advisors from outside your agency who contributed to the analysis.

CEQ REGULATIONS

§ 1502.17 List of preparers.

The environmental impact statement shall list the names, together with their qualifications (expertise, experience, professional disciplines), of the persons who were primarily responsible for preparing the environmental impact statement or significant background papers, including basic components of the statement (§§ 1502.6 and 1502.8). Where possible the persons who are responsible for a particular analysis, including analyses in background papers, shall be identified. Normally the list will not exceed two pages.

Name	Contributions	Degree(s)	Years of Experience
Joan Ascher	Hydrology	BS Forestry MS Hydrology	8
David Buell	Soils	BS Soils	6
Susan Cassidy	Forestry/Editor	BA English MS Forestry	9
Edward Davies	Fisheries/Team Leader	BS Fish Biology	10

EXAMPLE 5.2—*Besides satisfying the CEQ requirement, a comprehensive list of preparers helps make the EIS or EA credible.*

List of Agencies, Organizations, and Persons to Whom Copies of the Statement Are Sent (Chapter 6.0)

Suggestions for Writing

NOTE: The following suggestions do not attempt to reflect the use of e-mail or the internet to communicate with various publics. As appropriate, check with your legal counsel if you want to use electronic tools to track either comments during scoping or comments on a DEIS.

CEQ Regulations

§ 1502.19 Circulation of the environmental impact statement.

Agencies shall circulate the entire draft and final environmental impact statements except for certain appendices as provided in § 1502.18(d) and unchanged statements as provided in § 1503.4(c). However, if the statement is unusually long, the agency may circulate the summary instead, except that the entire statement shall be furnished to:

(a) Any Federal agency which has jurisdiction by law or special expertise with respect to any environmental impact involved and any appropriate Federal, State, or local agency authorized to develop and enforce environmental standards.
(b) The applicant, if any.
(c) Any person, organization, or agency requesting the entire environmental impact statement.
(d) In the case of a final environmental impact statement any person, organization, or agency which submitted substantive comments on the draft.

If the agency circulates the summary and thereafter receives a timely request for the entire statement and for additional time to comment, the time for that requestor only shall be extended by at least 15 days beyond the minimum period.

6.0 List of Agencies, Organizations, and Persons to Whom Copies of the Statement Are Sent

6.1 Keep an orderly list of all agencies, organizations, and persons to whom copies of the EIS are sent. As noted in CEQ § 1502.19, you must circulate copies to certain Federal, State, and local agencies, as well as to any members of the public who have been involved in the process.

This list by itself is sometimes the sole content of Chapter 6. See example 6.1.

6.2 For both an EIS and EA, maintain a complete list of all people who contribute any information to the project or who inquire about the project. These people should always get a copy of the EIS.

Agency or departmental policy should guide you about the need to circulate an EA to the public. In some cases, only a copy of the Finding of No Significant Impact goes to the public.

6.3 For an EA, change the chapter title to "List of Agencies and Persons Consulted." Do not confuse this list with the list of preparers. The list in this chapter includes agencies and persons **outside** the agency writing the EA.

6.4 (Optional) Summarize your scoping process and reference the public involvement information in your analysis file. This summary reminds reviewers (and perhaps the courts) that you did make adequate attempts to notify the public and any interested agencies and parties.

As in example 6.4, you might include a variety of information besides a circulation list:

- Consultation and coordination with other Federal or state agencies

- Public participation

- Issues eliminated from detailed analysis

- Distribution list for the Draft EIS or EA and FONSI

6.5 Rather than summarize your scoping process in this chapter, you can include scoping information in an appendix or in the analysis file. The CEQ Regulations make no recommendations as to where you should summarize your scoping.

6.0 List of Agencies, Organizations, and Persons Receiving the Draft EIS

As part of the CEQ Regulations on the National Environmental Policy Act, the FWS (Fish and Wildlife Service) is circulating the Draft EIS to the following agencies, organizations, and individuals.

Those receiving the Draft EIS have 60 days to comment on the EIS. Their comments should be as substantive as possible. According to the CEQ Regulations (§ 1503.4), the Fish and Wildlife Service must respond in writing to every comment, even if such a response necessitates substantial changes to the EIS, such as the addition or deletion of alternatives or the analysis of new resource issues. The FWS will publish its responses along with the revised Final EIS.

EXAMPLE **6.1**—*Circulation of the DEIS is a primary tool for the agency to use as part of its NEPA disclosure actions.*

CHAPTER 6. CONSULTATION WITH OTHERS—PUBLIC INVOLVEMENT PROCESS

The chief purpose of this chapter is to list those agencies, organizations, and persons who were consulted in the EIS process and to outline the public involvement process. Because the FEIS, however, analyzes a project covered in a prior EA (Environmental Assessment), the parties involved in the original EA are also listed. Also important are those individuals attending the public scoping meeting. This chapter, therefore, has four sections:

- A list of parties who contributed information and views to the EA
- A list of parties attending the public scoping meeting held in Sonora, California, on September 15, 1997
- A list of agencies, organizations, and persons to whom the draft EIS will be or has been sent
- Public involvement process

EXAMPLE **6.4**—*Nowhere in the CEQ outline for EISs is there a discussion of scoping. Many agencies, therefore, include it in this chapter of the EIS.*

APPENDICES

SUGGESTIONS FOR WRITING

Appendix

1. Limit appendices to material that is indeed essential to the EIS or EA. One test is that the appendices should not contain material just pulled from the files; instead, include reports or data prepared just for the EIS or EA.

 See *FCSG—Appendices*

2. Use contrastive numbering systems for the main chapters and the appendices. So, if the chapters are called 1, 2, etc., then the appendices should be called A, B, etc.

3. Number the appendices using the appendix number and then the page number from that appendix: B–3, B–4, etc.

4. *Appendices* and *appendixes* are both accepted spellings. We retain *appendices* on this page because CEQ Regulations uses this spelling in its list of recommended format items (CEQ § 1502.10). The *U.S. Government Style Manual* (1984) prefers the spelling *appendixes*.

CEQ REGULATIONS

§ 1502.18 Appendix.

If any agency prepares an appendix to an environmental impact statement the appendix shall:

(a) Consist of material prepared in connection with an environmental impact statement (as distinct from material which is not so prepared and which is incorporated by reference (§ 1502.21)).

(b) Normally consist of material which substantiates any analysis fundamental to the impact statement.

(c) Normally be analytic and relevant to the decision to be made.

(d) Be circulated with the environmental impact statement or be readily available on request.

INDEX

SUGGESTIONS FOR WRITING

Index

1. All EISs must include an index, as illustrated in example 1. An EA does not need to have an index, and one is rarely required unless the EA is long (40 pages plus) or especially complex.

     See *FCSG—Indexes*

2. If possible, use a computer to help you alphabetize your entries. Be sure, however, that your final index reflects the final pagination of the printed EIS/EA.

3. Make the index detailed enough so that it is actually useful to readers. For example, **include citations to all relevant issues, to all other resources, to NEPA terms used, and to agencies and groups involved with the proposed action**. An index this detailed will be more helpful to readers than an index that only cites major headings (as in a table of contents).

4. Include *See* and *Also see* references to help readers locate related information. A *See* reference tells readers to go to another entry in the index. *Also see* reminds readers to check related information.

CEQ REGULATIONS

Index.

The CEQ Regulations (§ 1502.10) require that an index be prepared for all EISs. However, the Regulations do not state how the index should be written.

Action 1–3, 2–4, 4–17, 4–2. *Also see* Proposed Action
Affected environment (Chapter 3) 3–1 to 3–7
Air quality 3–4, 4–4, 4–8, 4–12, 4–17
Alternatives 2–3 to 2–8
    Eliminated 2–2
    Compared 2–10
Appeal rights iv
Aquatic organisms 3–2, 4–3, 4–8, 4–11, 4–16
Bighorn sheep 1–1, 2–3 to 2–8, 3–1, 4–1, 4–4, 4–7, 4–10
Black-tailed deer. *See* Sitka black-tailed deer

EXAMPLE 1—*A useful index is fairly detailed. Invest enough time to make the index a useful tool for readers. For example, subheadings under "air quality," "aquatic organisms," and "bighorn sheep" would make this index more useful. See the Index to this book for examples of subheadings.*

GLOSSARY (TERMS, ABBREVIATIONS, AND ACRONYMS)

SUGGESTIONS FOR WRITING

Glossary

1. Include a glossary for all EISs and for most EAs. A glossary is helpful because many readers of an EIS/EA are unfamiliar with agency and resource terminology. By including a glossary, you avoid having to include lengthy definitions in your text. You still may want to have informal (short) definitions within the text, leaving the longer definitions for the glossary. Glossaries occasionally appear at the beginning of documents, usually following the contents. Lengthy glossaries, however, will usually appear following appendices.

2. Include both resource terms and NEPA terminology in your glossary. Either within the glossary or in a separate list, explain all acronyms, abbreviations, and symbols.

3. As in example 2 of the *groundwater* definition, identify the sources of your definitions whenever possible.

CEQ REGULATIONS

No CEQ Regulations exist for the glossary.

4. Compile the glossary as you work on the project, not at the end. Technical specialists, for example, should contribute definitions of their terms when they turn in their draft materials. Such early submissions help eliminate conflicting definitions from different team members. Also, careful editing is only possible when the terms and their definitions are clear.

5. For repeated projects or similar proposed actions, prepare a single glossary for inclusion in every EIS/EA that your agency prepares.

6. For longer EISs, consider having both a total glossary **and** sub-glossaries throughout the EIS.

   For instance, you might include a brief glossary on hydrological terms as a lead-in to the discussions of hydrology in Chapters 3 and 4.

Groundwater

Water within the earth that supplies wells and springs. Specifically, water in the zone of saturation where all openings in soils and rocks are filled—the upper surface of which forms the water table. (From the *Wildland Planning Glossary*, USDA Forest Service General Technical Report PSW-13/1976)

NEPA

National Environmental Policy Act. This law, passed in 1969, went into effect on January 1, 1970. It requires all Federal agencies to disclose the environmental effects of their actions. The law also established the Council on Environmental Quality to implement the law and to monitor compliance with the law.

EXAMPLE 2—*Make your glossary complete enough to be helpful to the lay readers, especially readers unfamiliar with NEPA.*

BIBLIOGRAPHY

SUGGESTIONS FOR WRITING

Bibliography

1. Collect all bibliographic entries into a single alphabetical list. The information in this list will make full footnotes unnecessary; instead, use parenthetical citations when you reference sources. See example 1.

     See *FCSG—Citations*

2. Compile the bibliography as you work on the project, not at the end. Technical specialists, for example, should turn in bibliographic information along with their draft materials.

3. Make your bibliographic citations as specific as possible: author(s), date, full title (including subtitles), and the full source (edition, issuing group or press, and the city of publication). The format for this information, as illustrated in example 3, is fairly standard, but pick a format and use it from the beginning of your work on the EIS/EA.

     See *FCSG—Bibliographies*

4. Submit copies of all work cited when you submit your draft materials. For articles and short publications, submit clean, one-sided copies. For books, copy the pertinent pages or sections. These copies become part of the analysis file and are subject to copying, upon request. Do not rely on every team member keeping a file of their own publications cited.

CEQ REGULATIONS

No CEQ Regulations exist for the bibliography.

An exception would be common reference books or other readily available texts. The test is their availability at both reference libraries and the agency issuing the EIS/EA. Unless such references are widely available, include copies of the pertinent pages in the analysis file. Do not trust that you can locate such references after the EIS/EA is completed.

5. As in example 5, document carefully all informal sources—for example, personal letters and telephone calls. These should be included in the bibliography.

A recent survey of noxious weeds (Napier 1987, pp. 6–9) analyzed the economic loss to a typical sheep allotment from different types of noxious weeds.

EXAMPLE 1—*In many scientific publications, parenthetical citations are the preferred way to cite sources.*

Schwartz, Charles F., Edward C. Thor, and Gary H. Elsner. 1976. *Wildland Planning Glossary.* USDA Forest Service General Technical Report PSW-13. Berkeley, Calif.: Pacific Southwest Forest and Range Experiment Station.

EXAMPLE 3—*Make your bibliographic entries as complete as possible.*

MacMurphy, John. 1990. "Effects of Streamside Vegetation on Temperature." Personal telephone call, 24 May.

EXAMPLE 5—*Document even informal communication.*

RESPONSE TO COMMENTS

SUGGESTIONS FOR WRITING

Comments

1. Develop a procedure for handling comments even before you send out the Draft EIS. Usually, you should plan for the EIS team to be available to decide how to respond to the comments.

   For an EA, CEQ requires no comment period, so responses are not a formal requirement. Some agencies or departments do circulate draft EAs, but in these cases responses are handled informally.

2. Keep a clean master copy of all comments received and catalog all comment letters so that you can locate specific comments.

   How to catalog comment letters is always a problem. An alphabetical arrangement has advantages, but one disadvantage is that you can't finish arranging the letters until the last letter has arrived. An option is to number letters as they are received; then prepare a database cross-referencing the person commenting, the number of the letter, and the different problems or objections raised in each letter.

CEQ REGULATIONS

§ 1503.4 Response to comments.

(a) An agency preparing a final environmental impact statement shall assess and consider comments both individually and collectively, and shall respond by one or more of the means listed below, stating its response in the final statement. Possible responses are to:

   (1) Modify alternatives including the proposed action.
   (2) Develop and evaluate alternatives not previously given serious consideration by the agency.
   (3) Supplement, improve, or modify its analyses.
   (4) Make factual corrections.
   (5) Explain why the comments do not warrant further agency response, citing the sources, authorities, or reasons which support the agency's position and, if appropriate, indicate those circumstances which would trigger agency reappraisal or further response.

(b) All substantive comments received on the draft statement (or summaries thereof where the response has been exceptionally voluminous), should be attached to the final statement whether or not the comment is thought to merit individual discussion by the agency in the text of the statement.

(c) If changes in response to comments are minor and are confined to the responses described in paragraphs (a) (4) and (5) of this section, agencies may write them on errata sheets and attach them to the statement instead of rewriting the draft statement. In such cases only the comments, the responses, and the changes and not the final statement need be circulated (§ 1502.19). The entire document with a new cover sheet shall be filed as the final statement (§ 1506.9).

3. Appoint (or hire) someone to screen all comments for the various substantive points raised. Some comment letters may deal with a single problem; others will be shopping lists of problems and objections. As appropriate, catalog and cross-reference the individual points so that none is overlooked. If you receive many comments and if you discover duplications, consolidate the duplicates and develop a coding system. As noted above, you could then respond to a single comment once rather than repeat the response.

4. As in example 4, respond substantively and seriously. No matter how irrelevant a comment appears, respond to it

seriously. The person who commented should be able to track that the comment was received and to determine just what you (or the team) did about the comment. As CEQ § 1503.4 explains, your written response should clearly indicate any changes or adjustments the team decides to make in the issues discussed, the alternatives, or in the assessment of effects.

5. The response to comments section can appear as a separate chapter in the FEIS or, if necessary, as a separate volume.

Comment

"The Rubber Chicken timber sale will have a significant, adverse, and direct impact on a high-quality cold-water fishery. The DEIS notes the presence of the fishery but fails to give any meaningful consideration of the fact that the fishery, a prime recreational resource, will be effectively destroyed by the timber sale."

Response

The FEIS includes a more complete discussion of the possible connections between the Rubber Chicken timber sale and the fishery resources in Cross Creek. The fishery resources are profiled in the fisheries section of Chapter 3 of the FEIS (pp. 56–58). The Cross Creek fishery is currently being impacted by sediment. As the FEIS points out in Chapter 4 (pp. 134–135), natural erosion, summer-home development, existing roads, and the 1989 High Mountain forest fire are continuing to be the primary contributors to sediment into Cross Creek. According to the team hydrologist (pp. 134–135 and E–3), virtually no sediment from the Rubber Chicken timber sale would be delivered into the fishery section of Cross Creek. Consequently, the proposed timber sale will not contribute to the destruction of the trout fishery in Cross Creek.

EXAMPLE 4—*Respond substantively and politely, and be sure to reference sections or pages in the FEIS. As in this example, quote the comment unless it is lengthy; if lengthy, paraphrase carefully.*

Finding of No Significant Impact (FONSI) and Decision Notice/Decision Record (Optional)

Stand alone document

NOTE: The FONSI is a required NEPA document, according to CEQ § 1508.13. The FONSI follows an EA when the responsible official determines that impacts will not be significant.

For efficiency, agencies have routinely added additional decision language to the FONSI. Often this decision language has no separate heading (title). The Forest Service calls this decision language a Decision Notice; the Bureau of Land Management calls it a Decision Record. Usually a FONSI and Decision Notice/Decision Record are combined, but they could appear separately.

Agencies differ as to how to organize the FONSI and related decision language. Some begin with the decision rationale (suggestions A, B, and C below). Others begin with the FONSI (suggestions D and E below). Whichever organization you choose, record the legal FONSI clearly, as illustrated in Example 1–1.

Suggested Content

A. Briefly summarize the preferred alternative or proposed action: Explain **who** wants to do **what** and **where** and **why** they want to do it. Reference the attached EA, and explain where readers can obtain copies.

B. State the decision (if not clear in item A).

C. (Optional for a FONSI, but necessary in a Decision Notice or Decision Record) Give the rationale for the decision (selected alternative), including brief references to the other alternatives to help make the rationale clear.

D. Formally state the Finding of No Significant Impact (FONSI) as required by NEPA/CEQ.

E. List and discuss the reasons supporting the FONSI. These usually tie back to the issues (resources) listed as significant in the EA. Focus on the context and intensity of the impacts. Use CEQ § 1508.27 as a checklist for this discussion.

F. State, as applicable, any appeal or review rights and any associated deadlines.

G. State when the decision will be implemented. (Most EAs can be implemented as soon as the public is notified. However, under special circumstances implementation might be delayed.)

H. Type the signature block of the responsible official, including name, title, location of the office, and a place for the date.

I. (Optional) Include the name, title, phone number, and e-mail address of the agency representative who can answer questions about the EA.

> Based on the following summary of effects (as discussed in the EA), I have determined that Alternative 3, which I have selected, will not have a significant effect on the human environment. For this reason, no environmental impact statement needs to be prepared.

EXAMPLE 1–1—*Open the FONSI section with the legal finding. Follow up with supporting data and rationale.*

CEQ Regulations

§ 1508.27 Significantly.

"Significantly" as used in NEPA requires considerations of both context and intensity:

(a) *Context.* This means that the significance of an action must be analyzed in several contexts such as society as a whole (human, national), the affected region, the affected interests, and the locality. Significance varies with the setting of the proposed action. For instance, in the case of a site-specific action, significance would usually depend upon the effects in the locale rather than in the world as a whole. Both short- and long-term effects are relevant.

(b) *Intensity.* This refers to the severity of impact. Responsible officials must bear in mind that more than one agency may make decisions about partial aspects of a major action. The following should be considered in evaluating intensity:

(1) Impacts that may be both beneficial and adverse. A significant effect may exist even if the Federal agency believes that on balance the effect will be beneficial.

(2) The degree to which the proposed action affects public health or safety.

(3) Unique characteristics of the geographic area such as proximity to historic or cultural resources, park lands, prime farmlands, wetlands, wild and scenic rivers, or ecologically critical areas.

(4) The degree to which the effects on the quality of the human environment are likely to be highly controversial.

(5) The degree to which the possible effects on the human environment are highly uncertain or involve unique or unknown risks.

(6) The degree to which the action may establish a precedent for future actions with significant effects or represents a decision in principle about a future consideration.

(7) Whether the action is related to other actions with individually insignificant but cumulatively significant impacts. Significance exists if it is reasonable to anticipate a cumulatively significant impact on the environment. Significance cannot be avoided by terming an action temporary or by breaking it down into small component parts.

(8) The degree to which the action may adversely affect districts, sites, highways, structures, or objects listed in or eligible for listing in the National Register of Historic Places or may cause loss or destruction of significant scientific, cultural, or historical resources.

(9) The degree to which the action may adversely affect an endangered or threatened species or its habitat that has been determined to be critical under the Endangered Species Act of 1973.

(10) Whether the action threatens a violation of Federal, State, or local law or requirements imposed for the protection of the environment.

Nepa / CEQ / DOI / BLM

Cite #'s of involved people - user groups
Use as checklist

SUGGESTIONS FOR WRITING

FONSI (Finding of No Significant Impact)

1. The FONSI is a crucial legal finding by an agency's responsible official that no significant environmental impacts (effects) will occur. If the official cannot sign the FONSI, the agency has to prepare an EIS before taking any actions related to the proposed action.

   The FONSI is keyed to a subjective threshold of significance as determined by the responsible official, who must rely on the information in the EA (and all its supporting information). The agency has the legal burden to demonstrate that no significant effects are even likely. Thus, as the bar charts in example 1–2 indicate, the more uncertain the potential effects, the harder it is for the responsible official to sign a FONSI and the greater the agency risk (vulnerability).

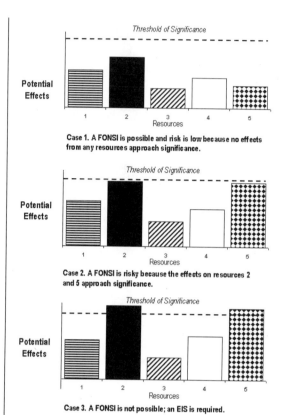

Case 1. A FONSI is possible and risk is low because no effects from any resources approach significance.

Case 2. A FONSI is risky because the effects on resources 2 and 5 approach significance.

Case 3. A FONSI is not possible; an EIS is required.

EXAMPLE **1–2**—*The more uncertain the effects, the more unlikely and riskier it is for the decisionmaker to sign a FONSI.*

CEQ REGULATIONS

§ 1508.13 Finding of no significant impact.

"Finding of no significant impact" means a document by a Federal agency briefly presenting the reasons why an action, not otherwise excluded (§ 1508.4), will not have a significant effect on the human environment and for which an environmental impact statement therefore will not be prepared. It shall include the environmental assessment or a summary of it and shall note any other environmental documents related to it (§ 1501.7(a)(5)). If the assessment is included, the finding need not repeat any of the discussion in the assessment but may incorporate it by reference.

2. Make the information in your FONSI as project- and site-specific as possible. Be especially careful to explain the impacts in terms of their potential significance (nonsignificance).

   FONSIs in the 1970s and the early 1980s were often very short and generic. Many FONSIs were even word-for-word identical, except for the name of the project and the signature and date. Such FONSIs have been increasingly hard to defend because they fail to show that the responsible official is signing the FONSI with a full and honest knowledge of all impacts, including the uncertainties related to environmental analysis.

3. Build in enough information from the EA so that the FONSI is essentially a stand-alone document. The FONSI becomes, therefore, a summary of the EA. See the discussion of the summary (pp. 14–15).

   As in examples 3–1 and 3–2, refer to specific pages and sections of the EA (or of the analysis file, if appropriate).

- Impacts on the sage-grouse strutting grounds in the project area will be minimal and not significant because only 15 percent of the existing strutting grounds will be temporarily affected (p. 19). These temporary effects will last no longer than two seasons. Also, the 15 percent estimate decreases to less than 1 percent in the context of the total sage-grouse habitat within the whole Cabin Creek drainage (p. 12).

- Potential significant impacts on water quality in Cabin Creek will be mitigated by (1) restricting construction activities to periods of dry weather and (2) building a holding pond for any expected runoff from the western part of the site. I am confident, based on the analysis in the EA (p. 22), that these mitigations will be effective.

- According to the EA (p. 7) and the supporting report prepared by the wildlife biologist, no threatened or endangered species occur in the project area.

EXAMPLE 3–1—*A FONSI should present the rationale for each of the decisionmaker's decisions.*

As the EA indicates (p. 8), only 5 percent of the elk herd will be affected, so impacts on elk will not be significant.

EXAMPLE 3–2—*Throughout the FONSI, refer to sections or pages in the EA.*

- Although wetlands are adjacent to the proposed campground, impacts on the wetlands will be avoided, primarily because the road corridor in the selected alternative avoids the wetlands (p. 6). Also, a key construction mitigation (barrier dikes at the boundary of the campground) will prevent any possibility of sediment or sewage from reaching the wetlands. See section 1508.27(b)(3).

- The Friends of the Sugar Pine (Friends) have been very concerned about the effects of the campground on the stands of old-growth sugar pine in and near the site of the campground. They have attended our public meetings and have met personally with me. We have addressed their concerns by designing the campground to retain key stands within the campground (p. 8); no stands outside the campground will be affected (p. 24).

  My judgment is that the Friends' concerns do not reflect a situation that is "highly controversial" as listed in section 1508.27(b)(4) of the CEQ Regulations. I recognize that the Friends are still not 100 percent satisfied, but they do agree that some of our design changes will mitigate the effects on sugar pine. Neither they nor other concerned publics have indicated that the construction of the campground is a highly sensitive (controversial) decision.

EXAMPLE 4–1—*Insofar as possible, reference in the FONSI § 1508.27 of the CEQ Regulations.*

- Of the 10 points under section 1508.27(b), the following ones will not be discussed further for these reasons: no effects on public health or safety; no unique geographic features (except for wetlands, as discussed above); no highly uncertain or unknown risks; no precedents for future actions; no cumulative effects (EA, pp. 26–28); no historic or cultural sites; no threatened or endangered species (Report from the wildlife biologist in appendix C); and no violations of Federal, State, or local laws.

EXAMPLE 4–2—*For completeness, be sure to mention (list) resources not affected.*

4. As in examples 4–1 and 4–2, use the information in CEQ § 1508.27 as a checklist and reference any pertinent items from that checklist as you prepare your FONSI.

   Those items from CEQ § 1508.27 that are not affected or even present should be summarized even if you can only assert that they are not pertinent.

5. Be sure to include in the signature block the full name of the signing official, the official's title, the location of the official's office, and the phone number. Also, include a line for the date the FONSI is signed.

6. If the FONSI circulates to the public without the EA or EA decision document, then include the name, title, e-mail address, and phone number of the person who could answer questions about the FONSI. Such information is a courtesy, even though not required by CEQ Regulations.

Cite page references in FONSI from EA.

RECORD OF DECISION

SUGGESTED CONTENT

A. State the proposed action: Explain **who wants** to do **what** and **where** and **why** they want to do it.

B. 1. State the agency's decision (that is, the selected/preferred alternative).
   2. State the rationale for its selection, including the major environmental reasons.
   3. Show how the selected alternative responds to the relevant issues (resources).
   4. Identify the environmentally preferable alternative(s).

C. Explain the major management (not only environmental) reasons that were used to select the preferred alternative.

D. Briefly summarize the other alternatives, and, as necessary, explain why they were not selected.

E. If not already discussed, state if "all practicable means to avoid or minimize environmental harm . . . have been adopted." Summarize any applicable mitigations. Also, summarize any monitoring and enforcement provisions.

F. State any appeal (review) rights.

G. State when the decision will be implemented. Usually, implementation can occur no sooner than 30 days after the EPA publishes a notice in the FEDERAL REGISTER of the FEIS being completed. Explain any delays due to other laws or agency regulations.

H. Type the signature block of the responsible official, including name, location, administrative unit, telephone number, and e-mail address. Include a line for the date.

SUGGESTIONS FOR WRITING

1. Include a careful rationale (explanation) of the reasons for the choice. As in example 1, the rationale should include different and conflicting opinions, especially as these relate to different points of view as to the significance of effects.

   Without a careful, comprehensive rationale, the decisionmaker could be accused of making "an arbitrary and capricious" decision.

2. List and explain any required mitigations essential to the intent of the preferred alternative. This list becomes the agency's commitment to the public as to what will be implemented.

   Realistically, some steps in implementation (and accompanying mitigation) may be contingent on budgets and other uncertain contingencies. Remember, however, that if the agency fails to implement a crucial mitigation, the agency may be forced to prepare a supplemental EIS to consider the changed and changing situation.

The preferred alternative provides access to the Lost Gulch Mine while not excessively impacting the bighorn sheep (Issue 1). The proposed mine access road will skirt a lambing area (one of six lambing areas within roughly 10 square miles). As the EIS (p. 167) indicates, use of this one lambing area by the sheep currently using it will decrease by 20 to 30 percent. This estimate by the wildlife biologist is based on the best available data, which is sketchy. (See p. 168 of the EIS.) Despite a low confidence level in regard to the data, I judge that the impacts on the bighorn sheep will not be significant because of the other lambing areas nearby. Even if the full 30 percent decline in use would occur in the one lambing area, the overall impacts on sheep at all six areas would be only about 5 percent.

EXAMPLE 1—*A carefully written rationale is the key to a good Record of Decision.*

CEQ REGULATIONS

§ 1505.2 Record of decision in cases requiring environmental impact statements.

At the time of its decision (§ 1506.10) or, if appropriate, its recommendation to Congress, each agency shall prepare a concise public record of decision. The record, which may be integrated into any other record prepared by the agency, including that required by OMB Circular A-95 (Revised), part I, sections 6 (c) and (d), and part II, section 5(b)(4), shall:

(a) State what the decision was.

(b) Identify all alternatives considered by the agency in reaching its decision, specifying the alternative or alternatives which were considered to be environmentally preferable. An agency may discuss preferences among alternatives based on relevant factors including economic and technical considerations and agency statutory missions. An agency shall identify and discuss all such factors including any essential considerations of national policy which were balanced by the agency in making its decision and state how those considerations entered into its decision.

(c) State whether all practicable means to avoid or minimize environmental harm from the alternative selected have been adopted, and if not, why they were not. A monitoring and enforcement program shall be adopted and summarized where applicable for any mitigation.

Note that the identification of the environmentally preferable alternative is necessary for an EIS in the ROD but unnecessary for an EA and the FONSI.

3. Clear up any potential confusion between the terms *preferred alternative, selected (chosen) alternative,* and the *environmentally preferable alternative.* As necessary, stipulate how you are using these terms.

- The agency should identify the preferred alternative in a Draft EIS (CEQ § 1502.14) if they have identified a preferred alternative. Identifying the preferred alternative is especially helpful because it tells readers which alternative the agency is likely to choose. Without this information, readers wouldn't know the agency's preference, especially because no draft Record of Decision is prepared.

- In a Final EIS, the preferred alternative is usually the same one selected (chosen) in the Record of Decision. The responsible official can, however, add or subtract actions and mitigations at the last minute, so the alternative selected (chosen) may be somewhat different from the preferred one identified in the EIS.

- The environmentally preferable alternative is that alternative that best satisfies section 101 of NEPA. This section of the law does not mandate that no impacts will occur, but it does indicate that the agency should carefully balance the different possible actions in order to best "fulfill the responsibilities of each generation as trustee of the environment."

NOTICE OF INTENT

SUGGESTED CONTENT

A. State the proposed action: Explain **who wants** to do **what** and **where** and **why** they want to do it.

B. Describe (if known) alternatives to the proposed action. If appropriate, refer to pertinent laws, agency missions, and other environmental documents, such as broad planning EISs that might influence the range of alternatives.

C. Summarize the agency's proposed scoping process, including (if known) the date and time of the initial public scoping meeting. This discussion would ordinarily include the names of cooperating agencies or other groups who will contribute to the EIS.

D. State the name, address, phone number, and e-mail address of the person within the agency who can answer questions about the proposed action and the EIS.

SUGGESTIONS FOR WRITING

Notice of Intent

1. The notice of intent appears in the FEDERAL REGISTER "as soon as practicable" after an agency knows that an EIS is required for a proposed action. See specific agency regulations for how to process a notice of intent.

CEQ REGULATIONS

§ 1508.22 Notice of intent.

"Notice of intent" means a notice that an environmental impact statement will be prepared and considered. The notice shall briefly:

(a) Describe the proposed action and possible alternatives.
(b) Describe the agency's proposed scoping process including whether, when, and where any scoping meeting will be held.
(c) State the name and address of a person within the agency who can answer questions about the proposed action and the environmental impact statement.

CEQ REGULATIONS

§ 1501.7 Scoping.

There shall be an early and open process for determining the scope of issues to be addressed and for identifying the significant issues related to a proposed action. This process shall be termed scoping. As soon as practicable after its decision to prepare an environmental impact statement and before the scoping process the lead agency shall publish a notice of intent (§ 1508.22) in the FEDERAL REGISTER except as provided in § 1507.3(e).

. . .

CEQ REGULATIONS

§ 1507.3 Agency procedures.

(e) Agency procedures may provide that where there is a lengthy period between the agency's decision to prepare an environmental impact statement and the time of actual preparation, the notice of intent required by § 1501.7 may be published at a reasonable time in advance of preparation of the draft statement.

2. An agency may delay publishing a notice of intent if it will not be preparing the EIS for a "lengthy period" (§1507.3(e)).

3. Include as much information in your notice of intent as you have available. Without sufficient background, readers of the notice of intent will be unable to respond with specific and substantial comments and questions.

    Many readers may be unfamiliar both with the project area and with the proposed action. These readers need detailed information in order to determine if they should even call the contact person for further information.

4. If work on the EIS ceases, a cancellation notice must be sent to the FEDERAL REGISTER. The cancellation refers to the original notice of intent and explains why work on the EIS has ceased.

CATEGORICAL EXCLUSION

NOTE: No consistent documentation requirements exist for categorical exclusions. Some agencies rarely document decisions that an action is a categorical exclusion. Other agencies merely use internal memos for categorical exclusions. The U.S. Forest Service is now requiring a specific document (Decision Memo) for certain types of categorical exclusions. The U.S. Air Force requires written documentation for only a few of its categorical exclusions.

SUGGESTED CONTENT

A. State the proposed action: Explain **who wants** to do **what** and **where** and **why** they want to do it.

B. Summarize any scoping and public involvement, including issues identified.

C. Explain why the proposed action is a categorical exclusion under agency procedures, which always list certain actions as potential categorical exclusions. Be sure to reference the specific agency guideline.

D. Explain that no extraordinary circumstances exist that would remove the action from consideration as a categorical exclusion. Such circumstances would include wetlands nearby, a cultural resources site, public health and safety concerns, controversial effects, or a threatened or endangered species.

E. Summarize findings or compliance with other laws or regulations. For example, if this categorical exclusion is tiered to an EIS/EA, consistency with that EIS/EA would need to be discussed.

F. State when the decision will be implemented.

G. State any appeal (review) rights.

H. Give the name, title, address, and phone number of the person to contact for further information.

I. Type the signature block of the responsible official, including name, location, administrative unit, telephone number, and e-mail address. Include a separate line for the date.

CEQ REGULATIONS

§ 1508.4 Categorical exclusion

"Categorical exclusion" means a category of actions which do not individually or cumulatively have a significant effect on the human environment and which have been found to have no such effect in procedures adopted by a Federal agency in implementation of these regulations (§ 1507.3) and for which, therefore, neither an environmental assessment nor an environmental impact statement is required. An agency may decide in its procedures or otherwise, to prepare environmental assessments for the reasons stated in § 1508.9 even though it is not required to do so. Any procedures under this section shall provide for extraordinary circumstances in which a normally excluded action may have a significant environmental effect.

SUGGESTIONS FOR WRITING

Categorical Exclusion

1. Even if your agency does not require documentation for a categorical exclusion, record appropriate background information supporting your decision to categorically exclude an action. Such records constitute the legal record if your decision is called into question.

2. All decisions to categorically exclude an action require an appropriate level of scoping. At the very least, the responsible official and appropriate staff determine that no extraordinary circumstances exist that would affect the following:

   • Public health and safety

   • Cultural resources or other unique geographic features

   • Highly controversial actions

   • Highly uncertain effects or unknown risks

   • Precedents for future actions

   • Cumulative effects that might be significant

   • Sites on or eligible for the National Register of Historic Places

   • Threatened or endangered species

   • Wetlands or floodplains

   • Any other resource impacts that might be significant

   This list or a similar one could go in the files as background to the decision that a categorical exclusion is appropriate.

3. As part of scoping, notify any nearby landowners or other potentially affected publics. Although CEQ does not call a categorical exclusion a public document, NEPA implies a minimum (appropriate) level of disclosure for a proposed action (even one that is categorically excluded). Be sure to keep careful records of all public contacts, even phone calls or incidental discussions.

   The U.S. Forest Service requires that the public be notified when a Decision Memo on a categorical exclusion is completed. Other agencies and departments have no required procedures for notifying the public about categorical exclusions.

ANALYSIS FILE (PLANNING RECORD)

The analysis file (planning or administrative record) is what an agency must rely on if it is challenged in court. Should litigation occur, the court will demand full legal disclosure of all records relating to the project being litigated. Too often, agencies have not kept very good records. At times, they have had almost no documentation except the EIS/EA.

The NEPA process is a complex documentation process. As such, the final EIS/EA and decision documents rely on each of the supporting documents. Each layer of documentation is important for the full legal record.

Agencies and departments have no consistent term for background NEPA material. Some call it the analysis file. Others refer to the planning record. Still others speak of the administrative (legal) record. Whatever the term used, the agency (and each interdisciplinary team) has an obligation to prepare a complete, well-indexed, and understandable file of materials as background for each EIS, EA, or categorical exclusion.

Can't add material after FONSI or ROD is signed

Always keep the original copies b file

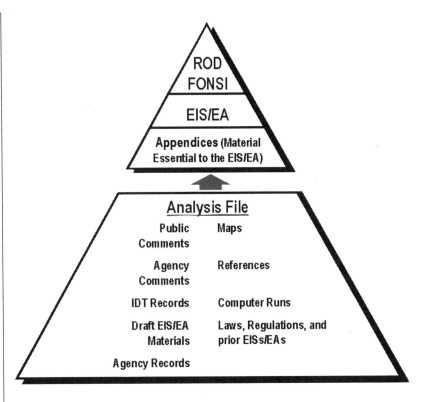

NEPA Analysis and Its Necessary Documentation

EXAMPLE—*The analysis file is the legal support for the EIS or EA.*

CEQ REGULATIONS

No CEQ Regulations exist for the analysis file.

SUGGESTIONS FOR PREPARING

1. The day an agency decides to launch a NEPA analysis is the day to begin preparing the analysis file. Any later is too late.

   Set aside a file drawer (or several), acquire several three-ring binders, and begin to collect materials related to the process.

2. How you organize (segment) the analysis file can vary, but you will likely have these general categories:

   • Public comments

   • Comments from other agencies and governmental entities

   • Interdisciplinary team (IDT) records

   • Other internal agency communication (non-IDT)

   • Draft EIS/EA materials (working papers)

   • Laws, regulations, and prior EISs/EAs

   • Maps

   • Computer runs

   • References (cited in the analysis file or in the EIS/EA)

3. Within each of these categories (segments), organize your documents chronologically (that is, either from latest to earliest or the reverse) and number them accordingly. Avoid using an alphabetical order because you will have to continually re-alphabetize (and renumber) as new materials come in.

4. Keep clean (unmarked), one-sided, 8 1/2- by 11 inch originals of every document included in the analysis file. Avoid handwritten, messy copies, which do not photocopy well; retype such documents, noting that the typed copy is a copy. Always retain the original however.

   Never let these clean originals circulate once they have become part of the analysis file. Instead, use these originals to make working copies as necessary.

5. As in example 5, keep a running (up-to-date) index of each document, including its number (in the analysis file), date, source (author), recipient, key content, and (if applicable) Freedom of Information (FOI) status.

   Your index can be as simple as the table of contents for each segment of the analysis file. Or you can develop a computer database, which will allow for quick access and retrieval. Either way, you need to have a system for locating all information in the analysis file.

6. Retain for the analysis file all formal and informal documents relating to the NEPA process. Informal documents include attendee lists from meetings, telephone logs, speed memos, and other documentation devices. **Always date and identify each item.** Also, note whether the document is a draft or working copy.

7. Discard items if they are clearly not part of the analysis process. For example, revised drafts of earlier drafts may not be greatly different; you need not retain each and every draft. Not all preliminary computer runs are important to the analysis; some of them may even be misleading, especially if the assumptions behind them were erroneous. Not all IDT communication is pertinent; be sure to date and explain any misleading and cryptic information you decide to retain from IDT deliberations.

   Technical specialists (team members) should not retain informal memos in their computer files unless they want (intend) them to become part of the legal record. In the event of litigation, such memos would be subpoenaed.

File No.	Date	Source	Recipient	Title and Key Content	FOI Status
B #12	8/13/91	BLM	T. Frank	Grazing Report for the Firestone Allotment	Open
C #5	6/15/91	IDT	—	Minutes (Alternative Formulation)	Open

EXAMPLE 5—*Develop a system for tracking documents in the analysis as they are submitted.*

8. The analysis file (including all individual and team computer files) should be frozen, usually on the date when the responsible official signs the decision document (Record of Decision or Finding of No Significant Impact). The reason is that the analysis should be an accurate record of what the responsible official used to make the decision. New and additional material would be misleading and could prejudice legal proceedings.

9. Keep all documents that are exempt from Freedom of Information requests in a separate locked file. Such documents would include proprietary mining data, location maps of cultural sites, sensitive threatened and endangered species information, and internal legal advice. Unless you keep these separate, you run the risk of sending them out to the public without knowing it.

   Note that some threatened and endangered species information may not be exempt; when you hear questions about the exempt status, check with your legal counsel.

Pre-decisional documents are usually not subject to Freedom of Information requests. Check with your legal counsel if you need to clarify the status of a particular document.

10. Retain the analysis file at least until implementation has ceased, including the time required for any follow-up monitoring. Beyond this time, agency policies should guide how long you retain analysis files.

APPENDIX A—SAMPLE OUTLINES FOR AN EIS OR EA

Chapters 3 and 4 of the CEQ recommended outline for EISs or EAs are often difficult to organize. The more issues and the more alternatives presented in the EIS/EA, the greater the number of subheadings needed. These subheadings, often capturing fifth- and sixth-level divisions in the content, are important content signals to readers. Their very number, however, can be distracting and confusing.

The following three examples show different ways to organize and number the parallel information in Chapters 3 and 4. As in these examples, your subheadings should be project specific, reflecting the significant issues you've identified and your alternatives. Given this project-specific requirement, no generic presentation of headings for these two chapters is possible. Only after you know the details of your proposed action and alternatives can you develop the headings and subheadings for these two chapters.

EXAMPLE A

3.0 Affected Environment

. . . .

3.6 Cultural and Paleontological Resources (Issue 5)

3.6.1 Prehistoric Resources

3.6.2 Historic Resources

3.6.3 Native American Resources

3.6.4 Paleontological Resources

3.6.5 Criteria for Significance of Impact Determination

Example A shows how the topics in Chapter 3 parallel the subsections presented in Chapter 4. In this example, Chapter 4 is organized using alternatives as primary divisions, with each resource (issue) presented under each alternative. The Shipley Group recommends this organization only when the EIS/EA is relatively short and uncomplicated. Otherwise, make resources (issues) your primary divisions in Chapter 4, with every alternative presented under each issue. (See pages 46–48.) See example C for an illustration of resources as the primary divisions in Chapter 4.

4.0 Environmental Consequences

4.1 Effects of Alternative 1—No Action

. . . .

4.1.6 Effects of Alternative 1 on Cultural and Paleontological Resources (Issue 5)

4.1.6.1 Prehistoric Resources

4.1.6.2 Historic Resources

4.1.6.3 Native American Resources

4.1.6.4 Paleontological Resources

4.1.6.5 Mitigation Measures and Their Effectiveness

. . . .

4.2 Effects of Alternative 2—Proposed Action

. . . .

4.2.6 Effects of Alternative 2 on Cultural and Paleontological Resources (Issue 5)

4.2.6.1 Prehistoric Resources

4.2.6.2 Historic Resources

4.2.6.3 Native American Resources

4.2.6.4 Paleontological Resources

4.2.6.5 Mitigation Measures and Their Effectiveness

The Shipley Group, Inc.

EXAMPLE B

Fish Habitat (Issue 3)

TERMS USED IN THE FISH HABITAT ANALYSIS

PRESENT CONDITION AND EFFECTS OF PAST ACTIONS ON FISH HABITAT (Issue 3)

Scope of the Analysis

Past Actions that Have Affected the Present Condition

Present Condition of Fish Habitat

Present Conditions of Fish Populations

DIRECT AND INDIRECT EFFECTS ON FISH HABITAT (Issue 3)

Scope of the Analysis

Direct Effects on Fish Habitat

Indirect Effects on Fish Habitat

Accelerated Sedimentation Rates

Number of Road Stream Crossings

Effects on Fisheries-Related Jobs

CUMULATIVE EFFECTS ON FISH HABITAT (Issue 3)

Scope of the Analysis

Past Activities and Their Effects on Fish Habitat

Present Activities and Their Effects on Fish Habitat

Proposed Activities and Their Effects on Fish Habitat

Example B shows how information from Chapters 3 and 4 can be combined into a single discussion. If Chapters 3 and 4 are combined, the major chapter divisions are usually resources (issues), with alternatives becoming subheadings under the resources.

Example B also illustrates the use of format options (type size, bolding, and indentations) to replace a numbering system.

The cumulative effects will often be only a summary of the preceding disscussions. Retain, however, the separate heading for cumulative effects.

This summary of effects may be necessary if this section on fish habitat is extensive. Otherwise, omit this summary.

SUMMARY OF DIRECT, INDIRECT, AND CUMULATIVE EFFECTS (Issue 3)

Alternative 1

Alternative 2

Alternative 3

Alternative 4

Alternative 5

MITIGATION MEASURES FOR FISH HABITAT AND THEIR EFFECTIVENESS (Issue 3)

IRREVERSIBLE OR IRRETRIEVABLE COMMITMENTS OF FISH HABITAT (Issue 3)

Example C

3.0 Affected Environment

. . . .

3.6 Socioeconomic conditions (Issue 4)

3.6.1 Population density and distribution

3.6.2 Economic conditions

3.6.3 Community services

3.6.3.1 Housing

3.6.3.2 Public-water treatment

3.6.3.3 Waste-water treatment

3.6.3.4 Solid waste disposal

3.6.3.5 Public safety

3.6.3.6 Health care and social services

3.6.3.7 Public schools

3.6.3.8 Local transportation

3.6.4 Social conditions

3.6.5 Fiscal conditions and government structure

3.6.6 Affected Indian tribes and their reservation settings

Example C shows how numerous subheadings can become when an issue is complex, thus requiring many subheadings to cover all of the subtopics. This example becomes more complex given the number of alternatives discussed.

Thus, if you can limit the number of your alternatives, do so. For similar reasons, concentrate on relevant issues and only selected indicators for these issues.

4.0 Environmental Consequences

. . . .

4.6 Effects on socioeconomic conditions (Issue 4)

4.6.1 Effects on population density and distribution

4.6.1.1 Effects of Alternative 1 (No Action)

4.6.1.2 Effects of Alternative 2 (Proposed Action)

4.6.1.3 Effects of Alternative 3

4.6.1.4 Effects of Alternative 4

4.6.2 Effects on economic conditions

4.6.2.1 Effects of Alternative 1 (No Action)

4.6.2.2 Effects of Alternative 2 (Proposed Action)

4.6.2.3 Effects of Alternative 3

4.6.2.4 Effects of Alternative 4

4.6.3 Effects on community services

4.6.3.1 Housing

Effects of Alternative 1 (No Action)

Effects of Alternative 2 (Proposed Action)

Effects of Alternative 3

Effects of Alternative 4

4.6.3.2 Public-water treatment

Effects of Alternative 1 (No Action)

Effects of Alternative 2 (Proposed Action)

Effects of Alternative 3

Effects of Alternative 4

The effects of each alternative would be further divided into direct, indirect, and cumulative. These categories (topics) might not require, however, separate numbered subheadings.

The key Chapter 4 requirement is that the effects of each alternative be trackable. For this reason, you should usually retain the subheadings even when several alternatives have identical effects.

4.6.3.3 Waste-water treatment

Effects of Alternative 1 (No Action)

Effects of Alternative 2 (Proposed Action)

Effects of Alternative 3

Effects of Alternative 4

4.6.3.4 Solid waste disposal

Effects of Alternative 1 (No Action)

Effects of Alternative 2 (Proposed Action)

Effects of Alternative 3

Effects of Alternative 4

4.6.3.5 Public safety

Effects of Alternative 1 (No Action)

Effects of Alternative 2 (Proposed Action)

Effects of Alternative 3

Effects of Alternative 4

4.6.3.6 Health care and social services

Effects of Alternative 1 (No Action)

Effects of Alternative 2 (Proposed Action)

Effects of Alternative 3

Effects of Alternative 4

4.6.3.7 Public schools

Effects of Alternative 1 (No Action)

Effects of Alternative 2 (Proposed Action)

Effects of Alternative 3

Effects of Alternative 4

4.6.3.8 Local transportation

Effects of Alternative 1 (No Action)

Effects of Alternative 2 (Proposed Action)

Effects of Alternative 3

Effects of Alternative 4

4.6.4 Effects on social conditions

4.6.4.1 Effects of Alternative 1 (No Action)

4.6.4.2 Effects of Alternative 2 (Proposed Action)

4.6.4.3 Effects of Alternative 3

4.6.4.4 Effects of Alternative 4 (No Action)

4.6.5 Effects on fiscal conditions and government structure

4.6.5.1 Effects of Alternative 1 (No Action)

4.6.5.2 Effects of Alternative 2 (Proposed Action)

4.6.5.3 Effects of Alternative 3

4.6.5.4 Effects of Alternative 4

4.6.6 Effects on affected Indian tribes and their reservation settings

4.6.6.1 Effects of Alternative 1 (No Action)

4.6.6.2 Effects of Alternative 2 (Proposed Action)

4.6.6.3 Effects of Alternative 3

4.6.6.4 Effects of Alternative 4

APPENDIX B—A COMPLIANCE CHECKLIST FOR AN EIS OR EA

The EIS/EA checklist on pages B–2 through B–5 is keyed to the CEQ Regulations. Thus, the checklist presents the legal minimums for an adequate EIS or EA.

The Shipley Group suggestions in the preceding pages are consistent with the CEQ Regulations as presented in the EIS/EA checklist. You should be aware, however, that this checklist does not include every suggestion or technique presented in *How to Write Quality EISs and EAs*. The Shipley suggestions, especially those that go beyond the CEQ minimums, are intended to help agencies or departments more effectively disclose the potential environmental effects of their actions while still complying fully with the CEQ Regulations.

Every Federal agency or department and even many district or regional offices have their own preferences as to what an acceptable EIS or EA should look like. The EIS/EA checklist is, therefore, a good starting point for a legal review of an EIS or EA, but the checklist will not cover every item an agency or department considers desirable.

EA/EIS Checklist (CEQ Regulations)

Document _____
Reviewer _____ Date _____

	CEQ Reference	Covered	Not Adequately Covered	Not Covered	Not Required	Remarks
Cover Sheet (not to exceed 1 page—optional for EAs):	1502.11					
List of responsible agencies, including lead agency and any cooperating agencies.						
Title of proposed action (and, if appropriate, titles of related cooperating agency actions) together with State(s) and county(ies) where action is located.						
Name, address, e-mail address, and telephone number of a contact person.						
Identification of type of document (EA, DEIS, FEIS, etc.).						
A one-paragraph abstract of document.						
More comments must be received by __(date)__ (Draft EIS only).						
Summary (Optional for EAs):	1502.12					
Adequately and accurately summarizes statement or assessment.						
Stresses:						
Purpose and need for agency action.						
Major conclusions (especially environmental impacts of all alternatives).						
Areas of controversy.						
Issues raised by agencies and public.						
Issues to be resolved.						
Choice among alternatives and identification of the preferred alternative (in an EIS).						
Does not exceed 15 pages.						
1.0 Purpose and Need	1502.13					
Briefly specify underlying purpose and need to which agency is responding in proposing alternatives including proposed action.						
2.0 Alternatives Including the Proposed Action	1502.14					
Based on information and analysis presented in sections on affected environment and environmental consequences, should present:						
Environmental impacts of proposal and the alternatives in comparative form.						

EA/EIS Checklist (CEQ Regulations)

	CEQ Reference	Covered	Not Adequately Covered	Not Covered	Not Required	Remarks
2.0 Alternatives Including the Proposed Action (cont.)						
Sharply defined issues.						
Clear basis for choice among options.						
Rigorously explore and objectively evaluate all reasonable alternatives.	1502.14 (a)					
For alternatives eliminated from detailed study, briefly discuss reasons they were eliminated.						
Devote substantial and equally detailed treatment to each alternative considered in detail including proposed action.	1502.14 (b)					
Include reasonable alternatives not within jurisdiction of lead agency.	1502.14 (c)					
Include no action alternative.	1502.14 (d)					
Identify preferred alternative (optional for EA).	1502.14 (e)					
Include appropriate mitigation measures not already included in proposed action or alternatives.	1502.14 (f)					
3.0 Affected Environment	1502.15					
Shall succinctly describe environment of area(s) to be affected or created by alternatives under consideration. (Shall be no longer than necessary to understand effects of alternatives.)						
Shall concentrate effort and attention on important issues; especially the presence or absence of the following potentially significant resources:						
Floodplains? [EO 11988; 10 CFR 1022]						
Wetlands? [EO 11990; 10 CFR 1022]	1508.27 (b)(3)					
Threatened, endangered, or candidate species and/or their critical habitat, and other special status (e.g., state-listed) species?	1508.27 (b)(9)					
Prime or unique farmland? [7 USC 4201]	1508.27 (b)(3)					
State or national parks, forests, conservation areas, or other areas of recreational, ecological, scenic, or aesthetic importance?	1508.27 (b)(3)					
Wild and scenic rivers? [16 USC 1271]	1508.27 (b)(3)					
Natural resources (e.g., timber, range, soils, minerals, fish, migratory birds, wildlife, water bodies, aquifers)?	1508.8					
Coastal zone areas [16 USC 1451 et seq.]						

EA/EIS Checklist (CEQ Regulations)

	CEQ Reference	Covered	Not Adequately Covered	Not Covered	Not Required	Remarks
3.0 Affected Environment (cont.)		/////////	/////////	/////////	/////////	/////////
Property of historic, archeological, or architectural significance (including sites on or eligible for the National Register of Historic Places and the National Registry of Natural Landmarks)? [EO 11593]	1508.27 (b)(3) (8)					
Native Americans' concerns? [EO 13007]						
Minority and low-income populations (including a description of their use and consumption of environmental resources)? [EO 12898]						
4.0 Environmental Consequences (forms scientific and analytic basis for comparisons under alternatives including proposed action).	1502.16	/////////	/////////	/////////	/////////	/////////
Shall consolidate discussions of these elements which are within scope of statement (should not duplicate discussions in Chapter 2.0 Alternatives Including Proposed Action Section).						
Environmental impact of proposed action and alternatives, especially the presence or absence of potentially significant resources listed above in Chapter 3.0.	NEPA (102(2)(C)(i))					
Any adverse environmental effects which cannot be avoided should proposal be implemented.	NEPA (102(2)(C)(ii))					
Relationships between local short-term uses of man's environment and maintenance and enhancement of long-term productivity.	NEPA (102(2)(C)(iv))					
Irreversible and irretrievable commitments of resources which would be involved in proposed action should it be implemented.	NEPA (102(2)(C)(v))					
As much detail about alternatives to the proposed action as is necessary to support comparisons of impacts.	NEPA (102(2)(C)(iii))					
Information about incomplete or unavailable information, including how such information might influence the analysis and conclusion.	1502.22					
Shall include:	1502.16	/////////	/////////	/////////	/////////	/////////
Direct effects and their significance.	1502.16 (a)					
Indirect effects and their significance.	1502.16 (b)					
Both beneficial and adverse impacts.	1508.27 (b)					
Cumulative impacts.	1508.7					
Possible conflicts between proposed action and the objectives of Federal, regional, State, and local (and in the case of a reservation, Indian tribe) land use plans, policies and controls for the area concerned.	1502.16 (c)					

EA/EIS Checklist (CEQ Regulations)

	CEQ Reference	Covered	Not Adequately Covered	Not Covered	Not Required	Remarks
4.0 Environmental Consequences (cont.)						
Environmental effects of alternatives including proposed action (comparisons under alternatives in Chapter 2.0, including the proposed action, will be based on this discussion).	1502.16 (d)					
Energy requirements and conservation potential of various alternatives and mitigation measures.	1502.16 (e)					
Natural or depletable resource requirements and conservation potential of various alternatives and mitigation measures.	1502.16 (f)					
Urban quality, historic and cultural resources, and the design of the built environment, including the reuse and conservation potential of various alternatives and mitigation measures.	1502.16 (g)					
Means to mitigate adverse environmental impacts (if not fully covered in Chapter 2.0 Alternatives Including the Proposed Action).	1502.16 (h)					
5.0 List of Preparers	1502.17					
Shall list names, together with their qualifications (expertise, experience, professional disciplines) of persons primarily responsible for preparing document or significant background papers.	1502.18					
6.0 List of Agencies, Organizations, and Persons to Whom Copies of the Statement Are Sent	1502.19					
Shall be sent to any of the listed groups or individuals, guaranteeing full and honest notification and disclosure.						
Appendices (Optional)						
Consists of material prepared in connection with the document (as distinct from material which is not so prepared and which is incorporated by reference).	1502.18 (a)					
Consists of material which substantiates any analysis fundamental to the document.	1502.18 (b)					
Analytic and relevant to decision.	1502.18 (c)					
Circulated with environmental document or readily available upon request.	1502.18 (d)					

Notes and Explanatory Comments (Whenever possible, tie comments back to evaluations in the preceding checklist.)

INDEX

Abstract, 12
Actions, 30
Administrative Record, 81–84
Adverse effects, 49
Affected, 36
Affected Environment (Chapter 3.0),
    3, 6, 36–45, A–1 to A–8
Agency
    comments, 81
    records, 81
Agency's preferred alternative, 5, 25. 34–35
Alternative considered in detail, 27, 30–31
Alternatives, 25–35, 76
    eliminated from analysis, 5, 25, 34–35
Alternatives Including the Proposed
    Action (Chapter 2.0), 2, 5, 25–35
Analysis
    boundary, 42–43, 49, 52
    file (planning record), 3, 81–84
    intensity, 49, 55, 71
Appeal (review) rights, 70, 75
Appendices, 3, 7, 17, 64
    (if any), 7
Appendix, 64
Assumptions, 49

Baseline environment, 36
Bibliography, 7, 43, 59, 67
Biological factors, 39–40

Cancellation notice, 78
Categorical exclusion, 79–80
CEQ (Council on Environmental Quality), 2
CEQ EIS/EA Checklist, B–1 to B–6
CEQ format, 2
Circulation of, 62
Comment letters, 9
Comments, 68–69
Commitments, irreversible and
    irretrievable, 6–7, 46, 60
Computer runs, 81–84
Conservation, 48
Contents, 16–17
Context, 42, 52–55, 71

Controversial effects, 74, 79–80
Council on Environmental Quality (CEQ), 2
Cover Sheet, 4, 9, 12–13
Cultural resources, 48, 55, 71
    or other unique geographic features, 80
    site, 79
Cumulative
    analysis, 52
    effects, 42, 49, 56, 80
    impact, 56
Cumulatively significant, 56, 71

Decision, implemented, 75
Decisionmaker, 20, 35
Decision Memo, 79–80
Decision Notice/Decision Record, 70
Decision(s), 4, 18, 20, 70, 75–76
Direct and indirect, 49
Direct effects, 48
Disclosure, 1
    summary, 3
Draft EIS/EA materials, 81

EA (Environmental Assessment), 2, 8
Economic factors, 40
Effects
    direct, 48–49
    indirect, 48–49
    on, 49
    uncertain, 56, 71
EIS (Environmental Impact
    Statement), 2
    checklist, B–1 to B–6
    circulation of, 62, 68
    format, 8
    supplemental, 75
Endangered or threatened species, 56, 71
Energy requirements, 48
Environmental Assessment (EA), 2, 8
Environmental Consequences
    (Chapter 4.0), 3, 46–60, A–1 to A–8
      (organizational option 1), 6, 46–47
      (organizational option 2), 7, 46–47
Environmental factors, 38–41

Environmental Impact Statement (EIS), 2
    circulation of, 62, 68
    format, 8
    supplemental, 75
Environmentally preferable alternative, 76
Existing environment, 36

Federal permits, licenses, entitlements,
    4, 18, 24
FEDERAL REGISTER, 2, 75, 77–78
Federal, state, or local law, 56, 71
FONSI (Finding of No Significant Impact), 14,
    21, 70–73

Glossary, 66
    of terms, 7

Headings, 16
Highly controversial, 55
    actions, 80
Historic resources, 48, 56
Human environment, 6, 56, 71

IDT (Interdisciplinary Team), 3, 10, 20, 22
    records, 81
Impacts, 50, 55
    adverse, 55, 71
    beneficial, 55, 71
Incomplete or unavailable information, 58
Incorporate by reference, 43, 59, 64
Index, 7, 65, 83
Indicators (quantification measures), 22–23, 49
Indirect effects, 48, 49
Intensity, 55, 71
Interdisciplinary team, 3, 10, 20, 22
Irretrievable, 60
Irreversible, 60
Irreversible and irretrievable commitments,
    6–7, 48, 60
Issue is relevant, 21
Issue-oriented EISs/EAs, 3
Issues, 18, 20–24

Laws, regulations, 81
**List of Agencies, Organizations, and Persons
    to Whom Copies of the Statement Are
    Sent (Chapter 6.0)**, 7, 62–63
List of Preparers (Chapter 5.0), 61
Location map, 7, 19
Long-term, 59

Management requirements, 28, 57
Maps, 7, 81
Matrix, 17, 31
Mitigation, 48
    measures, 26, 57
Mitigations, 5, 25–28, 57, 75
Mockup, 10
Models, 49
Monitoring, 28, 76

National Register of Historic Places, 56,
    71, 80
No action, 25–28
Nonsignificant, 24
    issues, 3
Notice of intent, 77–78
Number, 16
    pages, 16
Numerical ratings, 34

Objectives, 4, 18–19, 26–27
Organization (biological, economic, physical,
    social), 37
Outputs, 27, 31

Page layout (style sheet), 9
Parenthetical citations, 43, 59
Physical factors, 38
Planning Record, 81
Potential effects (impacts)
    adverse, 48
    beneficial, 48
    cumulative, 48
    direct, 48
    indirect, 48
    irretrievable (commitments), 48

irreversible (commitments), 48
long-term, 48
short-term, 48
Precedent for, 56, 71, 80
Preferred alternative, 26, 34, 75, 76
Project objectives, 19
Proposed action, 20, 25, 27, 28, 48, 75
Public
    comments, 81
    health concerns, 79
    health or safety, 79, 80
    involvement, 79
Purpose and Need, 2, 18
Purpose of and Need for Action (Chapter 1.0),
    4, 18–24

Range of reasonable alternatives, 5, 25, 30
Reasonable alternatives, 26
    not within the jurisdiction of the lead
        agency, 26
    outside the jurisdiction of your agency, 30
Recommended format, 8–9
Record of Decision, 75–76
References, 81
Relationship of short-term uses and long-term
    productivity, 46, 59
Relevant issues. *See* Significant issues
Resources, scientific, cultural, historical, 56, 71
Response to Comments, 68
Responsible official, 70, 74, 75, 80
Risks
    unique, 56, 71
    unknown, 56, 71
Rivers, wild and scenic, 55, 71
ROD FONSI, 81

Scope, 20, 26
Scoping, 4, 19, 21, 63, 77–78, 79–80
    information, 7
Section 101 of NEPA, 1
Section 1508.27 of CEQ Regulations, 71
Section overviews, 3
Selected (chosen) alternative, 76
Selection criteria. *See* Objectives

Short-term, 39
    uses and long-term productivity, 6, 59
    uses vs. long-term productivity, 49
Significance, 72
Significant, 56
    issues, 3, 6, 20–24, 26, 36
Significantly, 55, 56, 71
Site-specific, 27, 73
Social factors, 41
Substantive comments, 68
Summaries, 3
Summary, 4, 14–15, 73

Table of Contents, 4, 16–17
Technical assumptions, 49
Temporal boundaries, 53
Threatened or endangered species, 79–80
Tiering, 19, 29

Unavoidable adverse effects, 6, 46, 59
Uncertain effects or unknown risks, 80

Visual aids, 44

Wetlands, 55, 71, 79
Wetlands or floodplains, 80
Wild and scenic rivers, 55, 71